FREMDSPRACHENTEXTE

Morton Rhue

Give a Boy a Gun

Herausgegeben von
Herbert Geisen

Philipp Reclam jun. Stuttgart

This book is a work of fiction. Any references to historical events, real people, or real locales are used fictitiously. Other names, characters, places, and incidents are the product of the author's imagination, and any resemblance to actual events or locales or persons, living or dead, is entirely coincidental.

RECLAMS UNIVERSAL-BIBLIOTHEK Nr. 9111
Alle Rechte vorbehalten
Copyright © für diese Ausgabe 2003 Philipp Reclam jun. GmbH & Co., Stuttgart
Copyright © für den Text 2000 Todd Strasser (Pseudonym: Morton Rhue). Abdruck mit Genehmigung von Simon & Schuster Books for Young Readers, an imprint of Simon & Schuster Children's Publishing Division, New York
Seite 8: Copyright © 1999 USA TODAY
Seite 14: Aus einem Artikel in *The Christian Science Monitor*, 26. Mai 1999. Copyright © 1999 The Christian Science Publishing Society
Seiten 6, 21, 22, 30, 51, 69, 76, 79, 106, 112, 115, 153, 161: Copyright © 1998, 1999 New York Times Company
Seiten 24, 37, 41, 119, 123: Aus: Peter Wilinson / Matt Hendrickson, »Humiliation and Revenge: The Story of Reb and VoDkA«, Jann S. Wenner, »Guns and Violence: An Editorial«, in: *Rolling Stone*, 10. Juni 1999, sowie Randall Sullivan, »A Boy's Life«, in: *Rolling Stone*, 17. September 1998. Copyright © 1998, 1999 Straight Arrow Publishers Company, L.P.

Gesamtherstellung: Reclam, Ditzingen, Printed in Germany 2009
RECLAM, UNIVERSAL-BIBLIOTHEK und RECLAMS UNIVERSAL-BIBLIOTHEK sind eingetragene Marken der Philipp Reclam jun. GmbH & Co., Stuttgart
ISBN 978-3-15-009111-1

www.reclam.de

Give a Boy a Gun

Dedication

To ending youth violence.

To every young person who has ever been killed or wounded by a gun.

5 *To Kayla Rolland, age six, who was shot to death on February 29, 2000, in her first-grade classroom by a six-year-old schoolmate. The death of this innocent child will serve notice that we live in a country where gun use and gun availability is horribly, insanely out*
10 *of control.*

---

1 **dedication:** Widmung. 6 **first-grade:** Erstklässler- (*grade:* Klasse).
8 **to serve notice:** Kenntnis geben. 9 **insanely** (adv.): wahnsinnig.

Acknowledgments

My sincerest thanks to my editor, David Gale, and his
assistant, John Rudolph, for their insight and encour-
agement; and to everyone else at Simon & Schuster
for giving me the opportunity to write this book; to
Joanna Lewis Cole for her inspiration, suggestions,
and guidance; to Jann Wenner and *Rolling Stone*, and
Tom Diaz, for their dedication to fighting youth gun
violence and for their generosity; to Dr. Barry
Brenner of the Brooklyn Hospital / Cornell University Department of Emergency Medicine for his helpful information; to Sophie Ryan for her diligent re-
search assistance; to Erica Stahler for her excellent
copyediting; and to my family and friends for their
constant interest and support.

7 **"Rolling Stone":** amerikanische Musik- und Filmzeitschrift.
11 **emergency medicine:** Notfallmedizin. 12 **diligent:** gründlich.
14 **to copyedit:** redigieren, lektorieren.

Author's Note

One of the things I used to like about writing books
for young people was that it wasn't necessary to deal
with murder, adultery, and various other immoral
or criminal activities that seem mandatory in adult
novels these days. I find it sad and frightening that
this is no longer the case.

One of the things I dislike most about guns in our society is that, like violence and sex in the media, they
rob children of what we used to think of as a childhood.

The story you are about to read is a work of fiction.
Nothing – and everything – about it is real.

---

4 **adultery:** Ehebruch.   5 **mandatory:** unumgänglich.

"The hallways erupted in screaming, terror-stricken pandemonium as students realized this was ... another, increasingly familiar scene: a student with a gun."

USA TODAY, 5/21/99

1 **hallway:** Korridor. **to erupt:** explodieren. **terror-stricken:** starr vor Schrecken. 2 **pandemonium:** Chaos. 5 **"USA Today":** täglich erscheinendes US-amerikanisches Massenblatt.

8

Part of Gary Searle's Suicide Note

Dear Mom,

By the time you read this, I'll be gone. I just want you to know that there's nothing you could have done to stop this. I know you always tried your best for me, and if anyone doubts you, just show them this letter.

I don't know if I can really explain why I did this. I guess it's because I know that I'll never be happy. I know that every day of my life will hurt and be a lot more bad than good. It's entirely a matter of, What's the point of living?

Introduction

Around 10 P.M. on Friday, February 27, Gary Searle
died in the gymnasium at Middletown High School.
After the bullet smashed through the left side of his
5 skull and tore into his brain, he probably lived for ten
to fifteen seconds.

The brain is a fragile organ suspended in a liquid en-
vironment. Not only does a bullet destroy whatever
brain tissue is in its path, but the shock waves from the
10 impact severely jar the entire organ, ripping apart millions of delicate structures and connections. In the
seconds that follow, the brain swells with blood and
other fluids. The parts of the brain that control breath-
ing and heartbeat stop. One doctor described it to me
15 as "an earthquake in the head."

At the moment of Gary's death I was in the library at
the state university, where I was a sophomore studying
journalism. As soon as I heard the news, I went home
to Middletown, determined not to leave until I under-
20 stood what had happened there.

---

3 **gymnasium:** Turnhalle. **high school:** Sekundarschule (in den
USA), Gesamtschule (für die neunte bis zwölfte Klasse, gelegentlich
auch von der siebten Klasse an). 5 **skull:** Schädel. **to tear into**
s.th.: ein Loch in etwas reißen. 7 **fragile:** zerbrechlich. 9 **brain tis-**
sue: Hirngewebe. 10 **to rip apart:** auseinander reißen. 13 **fluid:**
Flüssigkeit. 15 **earthquake:** Erdbeben. 17 **state university:** (bun-
des)staatliche Universität. **sophomore:** Student(in) im zweiten Stu-
dienjahr; Schüler(in) im zweiten Jahr der Highschool.

Returning to Middletown was like stepping into a thick fog of bewilderment, fury, agony, and despair. For weeks I staggered through it, searching out other lost, wandering souls. Some were willing to talk to me. Others spoke because they felt a need to defend themselves even though no one had pointed an accusing finger at them. Some even sought me out because they *wanted* to talk. As if speaking about it was a way of trying to figure it out, of beginning the long, painful process of grieving and moving ahead.

Some refused to speak because it must have been too painful. For others, I suspect it was because they had learned something about themselves that they were still struggling to accept – or to conceal.

I spoke to everyone who would speak to me. In addition I studied everything I could find on the many similar incidents that have occurred in other schools around our country in the past thirty years.

The story you are about to read is really two stories. One is about what happened here in Middletown. The other is the broader tale of what is happening all around our country – in a world of schools and guns and violence that has forever changed the place I once called home. The quotes and facts from other incidents are in a different-style print. What happened in Middletown is in plain print.

This, then, is the story of what I learned. It is told in many voices, in words far more eloquent and raw than

---

2 **bewilderment:** Verwirrung. **fury:** Wut, Zorn. **agony:** Qual, Schmerz. 3 **to stagger:** torkeln, schwanken, taumeln. 14 **to conceal:** verbergen. 24 **quote:** Zitat. 25 **different-style print:** andersartiges Druckbild. 26 **plain print:** normales Schriftbild. 28 **eloquent:** beredt.

any I could have thought of on my own. It is a story of heartbreak and fear and regret. But mostly it is a warning. Violence comes in many forms – guns, fists, and words of hate and contempt. Unless we change the way we treat others in school and out, there will only be more – and more horrible – tragedies.

Denise Shipley

About Gary

Mrs. Searle and Gary moved into the house next to ours the day before second grade began. So the first time I actually saw him was at the bus stop. He was
5 kind of quiet, but friendly enough. Some of the kids at the bus stop would play soccer in the street in the morning. I was glad when Gary came along, because I wasn't into that, and with Gary there it gave me something to do. We'd mostly talk about stuff like
10 Magic cards and video games and what we saw on TV.

If you want to know the truth, I think Mrs. Searle was a little overprotective. I guess because she was the only parent. She always wanted to know where Gary
15 was going, and would he be warm enough, and junk like that. Gary would just roll his eyes.

Until Brendan came along, I think I was pretty much

Each day people wielding guns kill 64 people, rape 33 women, rob 575 people, and assault 1,100 more.

---

5 **kind of:** irgendwie.   6 **soccer:** Fußball.   8 **to be into s.th.:** auf etwas stehen, an etwas Spaß haben.   10 **Magic cards** (pl.): Sammelkartenspiel (Fantasy), bei dem es darum geht, die (Lebens-)Punkte des Mitspielers zu vernichten.   13 **overprotective:** überängstlich. 15 **junk:** Mist, Müll.
[Subtext]   18 **to wield:** schwingen.   19 **to assault:** angreifen.

Gary's best friend. The thing about Gary was that mysterious part of him that you never knew. It was like something he kept hidden and private. I can't explain it, but I could feel it when I was with him. He'd just get quiet and you knew he was a dillion miles away. I always thought maybe it was something about his parents getting divorced.

Ryan Clancy, a friend of both Gary's and Brendan's

Gary Searle was a very sweet little boy with slightly reddish brown hair and big, round eyes. He was polite and quiet and always did what he was told. I do recall that some of the children teased him about his weight. But you know how kids are at that age.

Ruth Hollington, Gary's fourth-grade teacher at Middletown Elementary School

I didn't move to Middletown until fifth grade, so I didn't know Gary before that. After we started hang-

---

"As parents, teachers, and other adults look for ways to reach out to young people, some see a common thread in the disappointments and isolation students experience when they lose a sense of place, lose a parental figure, or lose a girlfriend."

Christian Science Monitor, 5/26/99

---

5 **dillion:** etwa: Abermillionen, Zigmillionen.   7 **to get divorced:** sich scheiden lassen.   11 **to recall:** sich erinnern.   12 **to tease:** hänseln, aufziehen.   15 **elementary school:** Grundschule, Primarschule (für die ersten sechs bis acht Schuljahre).   17f. **to hang out:** (zusammen) rumhängen. [Subtext]   18f. **to reach out to s.o.:** (fig.) jdn. erreichen.   21 **parental figure:** Vater-, Mutterfigur.   22 **"Christian Science Monitor":** US-amerikanische Tageszeitung.

ing out, he'd sometimes talk about what it was like
when he was younger. About the divorce and how
completely nasty it was, and how after it was over, his
dad just left and never paid child support or called or
5 anything. That was a huge thorn in Gary's side. He
just couldn't get over that.

Allison Findley, Gary's on-and-off girlfriend at
Middletown High School

It was an ugly divorce. All that yelling and fighting.
10 Arguing over money. Gary was caught in the middle,
and sometimes I guess I used him to get what I
thought I needed. What we both needed. It's a terrible thing to put a child through, but I didn't know
what else to do.
15 *Cynthia Searle, Gary's mother*

Gary was enormously bright. You wouldn't know it,
because he was one of the quiet ones; never raised his
hand. I noticed it first in math. He almost always did
perfectly on his quizzes, unless he made a careless
20 mistake. But the computer was the real tip-off. I
wanted to do a class Web page. Gary volunteered to
do it. No matter what the problem, he seemed to
know three ways to fix it.

Stuart McEvoy, Gary's sixth-grade teacher at Middle-
25 *town Middle School*

---

4 **child support:** Unterhaltszahlung für ein Kind.   7 **on-and-off girl-**
friend: zeitweilige Freundin.   13 **to put s.o. through s.th.:** jdn. etwas
durchmachen lassen.   19 **quiz:** (Schul-)Prüfung, Test.   19f. **careless**
mistake: Flüchtigkeitsfehler.   20 **tip-off:** Tipp, nützlicher Hinweis.
25 **middle school:** Schule zwischen Grundschule und Sekundarschule.

A lot of kids play computer games and junk, but it
was different with Gary. The thing about him was he
was on [the computer] all the time. I'd call his house
and he'd answer with this faraway voice, and I'd know
5 he was online. He'd sound weird because there'd be
this split-second delay in his conversation, and those
typing sounds. Like he was doing two things at once.
Then one day I was over there, looking over his
shoulder. He had three instant message screens open
10 and was chatting with someone different in each one.
And he was on the phone. That's when I realized that
when I called, he wasn't doing two things at once. He
was doing four.

Ryan Clancy

---

15 "The outcasts, obsessed with violent video games and intrigued
by German rock music and Nazi culture, also had pastimes as
wholesome as baseball; they were part of a tight circle of friends,
earned top grades, held jobs and looked forward to life after
graduation – factors that no doubt reassured their parents."

20 *New York Times*, 6/29/99

---

4 **faraway:** weit entfernt.   5 **weird:** seltsam.   6 **split-second:** Sekun-
denbruchteil.   9 **instant message screen:** Bildschirmfenster zum sofortigen Austausch von Botschaften.   10 **to chat:** sich online unter-
halten.
[Subtext]   15 **outcast:** Außenseiter(in).   (*to be*) **obsessed with s.th.:**
von etwas besessen sein.   (*to be*) **intrigued by s.th.:** von etwas faszi-
niert sein.   16 **pastime:** Hobby, Freizeitbeschäftigung.   17 **wholesome:** gesund.   18 **grade:** Schulnote.   19 **graduation:** Schulab-
schluss, Abitur.   **to reassure:** beruhigen.   20 **"New York Times":**
angesehene, liberale US-amerikanische Tageszeitung.

I brought [Gary] to a psychologist. I hoped he'd let out a little of what he was feeling. She said he was guarded. I don't think she ever got close to what was going on in his head. It's obvious now that none of us
5 did.

Cynthia Searle

I'll give you an example of how bright Gary was. After the first month of sixth grade I got a message one day to call his mother at work. I remember the
10 phone call because she seemed reluctant to say exactly what was on her mind, but I finally got the impression that she was wondering why I didn't give more homework. Apparently, Gary rarely spent more than half an hour a night doing it. The funny thing
15 was half the parents in the class were complaining that I gave the kids too much homework.

Stuart McEvoy

It's easy to look back now and dissect the stuff you did for every little clue. Like one summer Gary and I
20 had these magnifying glasses, and we'd burn bugs and caterpillars alive. It was kind of cool to watch them twist and squirm. Is that a clue? Or something a dillion other kids do too?

Ryan Clancy

1f. **to let out:** rauslassen, preisgeben.   3 **guarded:** zurückhaltend.
18 **to dissect:** sezieren, auseinander nehmen.   19 **clue:** Anhalts-
punkt.   20 **magnifying glass:** Lupe.   21 **caterpillar:** Raupe.   22 **to
squirm:** sich winden.

I still find it difficult to believe he was part of what happened. The guns and holding those poor children hostage in the gym like that. What they did to that football player. That wasn't the Gary I knew. If you're
5 looking for answers, don't look at him. Look at Brendan Lawlor.

Ruth Hollington

2f. **to hold s.o. hostage:** jdn. als Geisel festhalten.   3 **gym:** Kurzform von *gymnasium*.   4 **football:** *American Football*.

Part of Brendan Lawlor's Suicide Note

To the good people of Middletown:

I hope this gets printed in big, bold letters on the front page of the newspaper, because it's something every
5 single one of you should read. I'm gone now, and you want to know why I took your kids with me?

Here's why. You made my friggin' life miserable. How? By the way you raised your kids to all want to be the same and to hate anyone who dares to be a little differ-
10 ent. Oh, no, you're probably thinking, you didn't do that.

You sure did. I've seen you in your cars staring at me and my friends. *Look at those creeps. Look at their clothes and the music they listen to. Why can't they go out for sports or at least root for our team?*

---

7 **friggin':** verdammt.   13 f. **to go out for sports:** Sport treiben.
14 **to root for s.o.:** jdn. anfeuern, jdm. die Daumen drücken.

About Brendan

Brendan Lawlor and his family lived here [in Springfield] until the middle of seventh grade [when they moved to Middletown]. I'd say from second grade on
5 I was about his best friend. There were times when we got into fights and wouldn't talk for a while, but mostly we were friends. I always thought Brendan was a really cool kid. Popular, too.

He was smart and funny and a pretty good athlete
10 for an average-size, thin kid. He was fast. He could really dis anyone to pieces, and he was one of those guys who would think up a cut-down right on the spot. I'll never forget one time when we were goofing on this one kid because he had B. O., and Brendan said, "Your
15 armpits smell so bad, the teacher gave you an A for *not* raising your hand." That really cracked us up.

Brett Betzig, a friend of Brendan's from Springfield

Brendan was one of the more vocal boys in the class, but also a very good student. He always had his

---

10 **average-size:** durchschnittlich groß.   11 **to dis s.o. to pieces:** jdn. fertig machen, auseinander nehmen.   **guy:** Typ, Kerl.   12 **cut-down:** verbaler K.-o.-Schlag.   13 **to goof on s.o.:** jdn. zum Narren halten, auf jdm. herumhacken.   14 **B.O.:** Abk. für *body odor:* Körpergeruch. 15 **armpit:** Achselhöhle.   **A:** beste Note.   16 **That really cracked us up:** Das fanden wir wirklich zum Schießen, da haben wir uns drüber totgelacht.   18 **vocal:** lautstark.   19f. **to have s.th. in:** etwas einreichen.

homework and projects in on time. He was very good at expressing himself on paper, although his grammar and spelling were atrocious, which is often the case with boys his age. He could be temperamental, but that's also not unusual.

Katherine Sullivan, Brendan's sixth-grade teacher at Springfield Middle School

You couldn't have asked for better neighbors than the Lawlors. Tom and Samantha Lawlor were so nice, always offering to help pick up a child or drive someone somewhere. They kept a neat house and a neat lawn, and I can count on one hand the number of times I heard either of them raise their voice to Brendan. I was very sorry when they moved away.

Kit Conner, a neighbor of the Lawlors' in Springfield

Brendan and I were on the same soccer teams because our dads were friends and they coached together. I was usually in a forward spot because I liked

---

"'[Mr. and Mrs. Kinkel] were devoted parents in a tight-knit family. ... Bill had tried everything with Kip.'"

A friend of the Kinkels', *New York Times*, 6/14/98

---

3 **atrocious:** entsetzlich.   17 **to coach:** (Mannschaft) trainieren.   18 **in a forward spot:** im Sturm.
[Subtext]   19 **Kinkel:** Der 15-jährige Kipland K. erschoss am 21.5.1998 seine Eltern und richtete danach in der Thurston High School, Springfield (Oregon), ein Blutbad an, bei dem zwei Schüler getötet und 22 verletzt wurden. Vgl. S. 171.   **tight-knit:** eng verbunden, gut zusammenhaltend.

to score. Brendan was usually on defense. He was
funny about soccer. Sometimes he'd race across the
field and throw his body in front of the ball like his
life depended on it, and other times he acted like he
5 couldn't care less. I always had the feeling his dad
wished he'd play harder and take it more seriously.

Brett Betzig

You know how some people seem really relaxed and
at ease with themselves? Not Brendan. He never
10 seemed comfortable. He was always a little on edge, a
little wary. It was like his brain couldn't stop, even
when we were just having a good time.

Julie Shore, a friend of Brendan's from Springfield

One thing about Brendan: He hated injustice. I re-
15 member there was this soccer game, and some kid on
the other team should have been called for hands. It
was really flagrant, but the ref didn't see it. A couple

"'Sue [Klebold] was more patient and gentle and kind with her
kids than I was able to be.'"

20 A friend of the Klebolds', *New York Times*, 6/29/99

---

9 (*to be*) **at ease with o.s.:** sich in seiner Haut wohl fühlen.   10 **to be
on edge:** nervös sein.   11 **wary:** vorsichtig.   16 **to call s.o. for s.th.:**
jdn. wegen etwas verwarnen.   **hands** (pl.): Handspiel.   17 **flagrant:**
offensichtlich.   **ref:** Kurzform von *referee*: Schiri, Schiedsrichter(in).
[Subtext]   18 **Klebold:** Am 20.4.1999 erschossen der 17-jährige Dylan K. und der 18-jährige Eric Harris in der Columbine High School,
Littleton (Colorado), 12 Schüler und einen Lehrer und verletzten 23
weitere Personen. Anschließend verübten sie Selbstmord. Vgl. S. 172.

of seconds later their team scored. Brendan went ballistic. He was right in the ref's face, shouting and cursing like a madman. The rest of us were actually embarrassed. Mr. Lawlor had to come out on the field
5 and take Brendan away. But Brendan just hated stuff like that.

Brett Betzig

I was out in the front of the house when Samantha [Lawlor] drove into her driveway and got out of the
10 car. She used to drive Brendan to school. This particular morning she looked like a wreck. Like she was going to cry. I asked if everything was okay, and she said Brendan had given her a particularly hard time that morning. I invited her in for coffee. I think she
15 was hoping that because I'd raised two sons, I could give her some advice.

She actually cried a little and confided in me that Brendan could be very difficult. He wasn't cooperative about doing chores, and he would blow up when he got
20 upset. She said there were days when it was practically impossible to get him out of bed and dressed for school. It seemed so odd to me. His parents were both the opposite – even-tempered. Samantha especially was soft-spoken and gentle. Maybe he was too much
25 for her.

Kit Conner

---

1 f. **to go ballistic:** ausrasten, in die Luft gehen.   9 **driveway:** Einfahrt.   11 **to look like a wreck:** elend aussehen.   17 **to confide in s.o.:** jdm. (etwas) anvertrauen.   19 **chore:** Hausarbeit.   **to blow up:** explodieren.   23 **even-tempered:** ausgeglichen.   24 **to be soft-spoken:** eine angenehme, leise Stimme haben.

We used to play video games a lot. One of our favor-
ites was *Need for Speed*. The idea was to win the
race, but we had just as much fun crashing into each
other and trying to run each other off the course.
Then Brendan got a demo of one of the *Doom* games.
I remember we were totally blown away by it. For a
couple of weeks it was all we did after school. And it
was only a demo. I remember Mrs. Lawlor coming
into his room one afternoon and wanting him to turn
off the game and go out and play. And it was like
Brendan didn't even hear her, he was so into that
game. She said it again, and Brendan told her to go
away. He didn't even look up. Mrs. Lawlor looked
totally stunned that he'd said that. Of course, Brendan didn't notice a thing. He was too busy playing.
But that was the only time I ever heard him be fresh
to her.

Brett Betzig

Though violent movies, music, and video games are popular in
many countries, few allow their citizens to own handguns. **In
1996, handguns alone killed 15 people in Japan, 30 in Great
Britain, 106 in Canada, and 9,390 in the United States.**

Rolling Stone, 6/10/99

4 **to run s.o. off the course:** jdn. aus der Bahn werfen.   5 **demo:** De-
monstrationsspiel.   **"Doom":** gewalttätiges Videospiel; wörtl.: Ver-
hängnis.   6 **to be blown away by s.th.:** von etwas begeistert sein.
14 **stunned:** wie vor den Kopf geschlagen.   16 **to be fresh to s.o.:**
pampig zu jdm. sein.
[Subtext]   20 **handgun:** Handfeuerwaffe.

The day [Brendan] found out he was moving he just looked terrible. I mean, at school he looked all pale and hollow and bent. I almost thought someone in his family had died. He really didn't want to go.

5   *Julie Shore*

The Lawlors were private people. Except for that one time with Samantha in my kitchen, she hardly ever said anything about [Brendan]. I'm not saying that's good or bad, but you had the feeling that if something
10 was wrong, they preferred to deal with it alone and not tell the whole neighborhood. Not that I ever had a reason to believe anything was wrong, other than what I already told you. But I do know that Brendan was very unhappy about moving. That's a hard age to
15 leave your friends.

                                                                                              Kit Conner

---

During the first half of the twentieth century the army trained soldiers to shoot at targets with bull's-eyes. The targets were changed to human forms after it was discovered that soldiers sometimes
20 couldn't shoot back in war even if their lives were threatened. **Military psychologists have noted that video games mimic military training designed to break down the inhibition against shooting human beings.**

---

3 **bent:** etwa: deprimiert, geknickt.   6 **private:** zurückgezogen (lebend).
[Subtext]   18 **bull's-eye:** Schießscheibenzentrum, das Schwarze.
21 **to mimic:** nachahmen.   22 **inhibition:** Hemmung.

Seventh Grade

Brendan seemed kind of lost when he first moved [to
Middletown]. It was the middle of the school year,
and here comes this minivan packed to the roof, and
5 about an hour later the moving truck shows up. The
moving guys started bringing furniture into the house,
and the family was kind of going back and forth too.
It must have been a weekend, because I went somewhere with one of my friends and his mom. I re-
10 member leaving my house and seeing Brendan out in
front of his house. He just stared at me. No hello. No
wave. No nothing. I think I kind of nodded at him
and then got into the car and left.
    A little later I come back. I'm getting out of the car,
15 and Brendan comes out of the house and heads straight
toward me carrying three tennis balls. So we start to
talk, and he's asking me what school I go to and what
grade I'm in and did I like this [video] game and that.
You know, kind of feeling me out. And all the while
20 he's juggling these tennis balls. It struck me as a little
bizarre.

*Dustin Williams, a neighbor of Brendan's in
Middletown*

---

4 **minivan:** Kleinlaster.   5 **moving truck:** Möbelwagen.   6 **moving
guys** (pl.): Möbelpacker.   19 **to feel s.o. out:** jdn. testen, sondieren,
aushorchen.   20 **to juggle s.th.:** mit etwas jonglieren.

26

I don't think he said a thing for the first two weeks. The only reason I even noticed him was because I sat in the back and he was back there with me in science and English. The way he looked, it was, like, wide-eyed – like a rain-forest dweller dropped into the middle of New York City. I bet three-quarters of the class didn't even know he was there.

Ryan Clancy

We started talking in the hall. I mean, I was hyper-aware of him because he was new and I was new, and your antenna is up for things like that. Like feeling all alone and trying to connect with someone you have something in common with, no matter what. It's like your boat just sank and you're in the water grabbing desperately for anything that floats.

Emily Kirsch, a former friend of Brendan's

I've always made a special effort with those [students] I sense are in distress. Believe me, no one comes into this school in the middle of the year without a lot of distress. After the first day of class I took [Brendan] aside and told him I knew it would be hard to adjust and that he should take his time and not worry too much. And I remember the way he looked at me. As if I'd caught him completely by surprise. He may have even blinked back tears.

Julia Reingold, a teacher of Brendan's at Middletown Middle School

---

4 f. **wide-eyed:** staunend.   5 **rain-forest dweller:** Regenwaldbewohner(in).   9 f. **to be hyperaware of s.o.:** jdn. überdeutlich wahrnehmen.   13 **no matter what:** egal was.   25 **to blink back tears:** Tränen unterdrücken, zurückhalten.

Here's this cute boy who didn't say a word for the first three weeks, but once he started talking, it could be hard to shut him up. At first all he could talk about was how big the school was and how much he missed all his old friends and his old school. I mean, I didn't mind it so much, because I felt like I was about the only person he had to talk to, and, frankly, I was in the same boat. But after a while it did start to get kind of repetitious, and I told him so. It was like day and night. After that, he never said a thing about his old friends or his old school.

Emily Kirsch

Each day fourteen children under the age of nineteen are killed by guns.

National Center for Health Statistics, 1996

---

1 **cute:** süß; schlau.   3 **to shut s.o. up:** jdn. zum Schweigen bringen.
9 **repetitious:** sich wiederholend.

Eighth Grade

I tried to think back to what it was like in eighth
grade. It was different. I mean, it got really cliquey.
But I think Brendan and I felt like, "That's okay,
5 we're new here. They just have to get to know us."
But it didn't work that way. They got to know us, but
nothing changed. Instead, this whole jock and cheerleader and designer name thing just got stronger and
stronger. They were like the Sun, and the rest of us
10 were all these little planets stuck in orbits around
them. After a while I think a lot of us didn't even
want to be in that [popular] crowd. All we wanted
was to be left alone.

Emily Kirsch

15 Things in school definitely changed in eighth grade.
At least for us guys on the team. Maybe it was because we knew we'd be in the high school next year.
Maybe it was that some of the guys were starting to
get bigger. Sometimes Coach Bosco would come over
20 [from the high school] and watch us. You know, like
he was scouting us for next year. It made us feel im-

---

3 **it got really cliquey:** da haben sich richtige Cliquen gebildet.   4 **I
felt like:** ich dachte so.   7 **jock** (infml.): Athlet.   7f. **cheerleader:**
Angehörige einer Gruppe von jungen Frauen, die beim American
Football die Mannschaften anfeuern.   8 **designer name:** Designer-,
Herstellername.   21 **to scout:** (aus)spionieren, aussuchen.

portant. All of a sudden we were aware that we were at the brink of a bigger world. Of course, it was just high school. But to eighth graders that was a big deal.

Dustin Williams

5 I don't think Brendan and Gary really clicked until around the middle of eighth grade, but once they did, it was like a lock. When I was hanging with them, I was definitely the third wheel. They were okay about it, but it was pretty obvious that I was just a visitor to
10 whatever part of their private world they wanted me to see.

Ryan Clancy

"Dylan Bennet Klebold grew up in a house without guns, even toy guns.
15 'Tom [Dylan's father] was adamant,' said ... a former neighbor. ... '[He said,] "We don't need guns in the house; we're not going to play with them."'"

New York Times, 6/29/99

---

2 **brink:** Rand.   3 **big deal:** große Sache.   5 **to click:** sich richtig gut verstehen.
[Subtext]   15 **adamant:** unnachgiebig, eisern.

Part of Gary's Suicide Note

I could have just gone and offed myself quietly, but that
would have been an even bigger waste. If I go this way,
taking the people who made my life miserable with me,
then maybe it will send a message. Maybe something will
change, and some other miserable kid like me somewhere will get treated better and maybe find a reason to
live.

Each year 2.5 million new handguns are sold in this country.

---

2 **to off o.s.:** sich ausknipsen, umbringen, erledigen.

More of Eighth Grade

I thought I knew Gary better. We sort of went together on and off for nearly two years. It's obvious
now that I didn't know him. Not really. I knew he had
5 that whole other thing with Brendan. Sometimes it almost felt like they had their own language. They each
just seemed to know what the other was thinking. But
now it's obvious he hid a lot. Not just from me, but
from everyone except Brendan.
10   *Allison Findley*

Until Gary came into the picture, I think I was Brendan's closest friend. I can't say I was really sorry
when that changed. By then I'd gotten to know some
other girls who were like me – quote, unquote "out-
15 casts" – and we were trying to have a life in spite of
all that cliquey weirdness at school. I don't know why,
but Brendan couldn't get past the weirdness. He was
more fixated on it. It was almost all he would talk
about. I was trying to get away from it. He just
20 wanted to keep looking at it under a microscope.
                                                     Emily Kirsch

Gary and I got into my mom's car one day. It was
parked in the driveway, facing the garage. Gary sat

---

14 **quote, unquote:** in Anführungszeichen.   16 **weirdness:** das Selt-
same.   18 **to be fixated on s.th.:** auf etwas fixiert sein.

behind the wheel, and I was next to him. He put his
arm around my shoulder, and we just pretended we
were driving somewhere. We were staring at the garage door with big flakes of white paint peeling off it,
5 but in our minds we were going through the desert.
Gary had done that once, so he was talking about cac-
tus and sun-bleached bones and jackrabbits and hot
sun.

I leaned my head on his shoulder, and I could see it
10 all in my mind. The two of us, all alone, driving through
the desert, a million miles away from everything. Just
sagebrush and creosote bushes and burned reddish
cliffs. A trail of dust flying up behind us. Gary pulled
me close and kissed my hair, and it was one of those re-
15 ally happy moments. I guess it was about as close as we
ever got to blissful puppy love. Ha, ha!

Then Gary stopped. I looked up and saw that he was
staring into the rearview mirror. I turned around, and
Deirdre Bunson and Sam Flach and a bunch of other
20 kids were in the street, pointing at us and laughing.

I wanted to die. Gary did too. He couldn't even turn
around. He just slumped down in the seat and stared at
that stupid garage door and the peeling paint. It was
like they'd just stuck a knife in his heart.

25 Sometimes Gary and I could escape into that world
where no one bothered us or laughed or made fun. But

---

4 **flake:** abgebröckeltes Stück.   **to peel off:** sich lösen.   7 **sun-
bleached:** sonnengebleicht.   **jackrabbit:** Eselhase (große, nordameri-
kanische Hasenart).   12 **sagebrush:** Salbeibusch.   **creosote bush:**
Kreosotbusch (heimisch im Westen der USA und in Mexiko).
13 **trail of dust:** Staubwolke.   16 **blissful:** glückselig.   **puppy love:**
erste Liebe, Schwärmerei.   18 **rearview mirror:** Rückspiegel.   22 **to
slump down:** (in sich) zusammensinken.

it never lasted long, and then it was like waking up from a dream and facing the cold, bald truth that it wasn't real and never would be. For the popular kids the dream was real. They lived it. They never had to be afraid of waking up.

Allison Findley

Ninth Grade

It started to change at the beginning of ninth grade. I
went away with my parents for two weeks in August,
and Brendan and Gary stayed home and just hung
5 with each other. When I got back, it was different. I
can't exactly explain how, but I felt it. There was
something dark in Brendan. I don't know where it
came from. Whether it had always been inside him, or
whether it just started to grow because of the way
10 people treated him in school.
                                                    Allison Findley

Gary wasn't always like that. When we were in eighth
grade and some big jock would body-slam us into a
chalkboard or rip the pocket off our shirt, we'd be
15 pissed, and we'd grumble about how we'd like to kill

"The … cliques that rule American high schools are every bit as
murderous as Harris and Klebold, only their damage is done in
slow motion, over a period of many years, and fails to draw the
attention of parents or teachers."
20   A posting on the Internet

---

13 **to body-slam:** (mit dem Körper) stoßen.   14 **chalkboard:** (Krei-
de-)Tafel.   14f. **to be pissed:** sauer sein, die Schnauze voll haben.
15 **to grumble:** murren, leise schimpfen.
[Subtext] 18 **slow motion:** Zeitlupe.   20 **posting:** (Internet-)Nach-
richt.

this guy and kick his face in. The thing was it was all sort of make-believe wishful thinking. Maybe you'd go home and play *Doom* for an hour and just blow everyone to bits. But you never *really* considered get-
5 ting a gun and going after them. At least, I didn't.

Ryan Clancy

Gary would try to play it down, make fun of it. He'd say, "Hey, doesn't matter, I'm just a loser." I'd tell him no, he wasn't a loser. But it was like he couldn't
10 hear me. The rest of the school said he was a loser, and that just drowned me out.

Allison Findley

People talk like our school is this sick, depraved place. That's so wrong. I talked to my mom and her
15 friends about it, and they say it was just like this when they went to school. It must be like this at every other high school. Yes, kids can be really mean to one another, really cruel. But that's the way it's always been. I mean, isn't part of growing up just learning to deal
20 with it?

Deirdre Bunson

Brendan and Gary got picked on. That's a fact. We all did. Little guys; fat guys; skinny, gangly, zit-riddled

---

1 **to kick s.o.'s face in:** jdm. in die Fresse treten. 2 **make-believe:** imaginär, Phantasie-. **wishful thinking:** Wunschdenken. 3 f. **to blow s.o. to bits:** jdn. wegpusten, kaputt ballern. 7 **to play s.th. down:** etwas herunterspielen. 11 **to drown s.o. out:** jdn. über-tönen. 13 **depraved:** verkommen. 22 **to pick on s.o.:** auf jdm. herumhacken. 23 **skinny:** dünn. **gangly:** schlaksig. **zit-riddled:** pickelig.

guys like me. Anyone who wasn't big and strong and on a team got it. You'd even see big guys on the football team push around some of the smaller players. Middletown High is big and crowded, and you've got
5 ten dillion kids in the hall at once. Maybe if it's an all-out, knock-down-drag-out fight, some teacher will notice and try to stop it. But if it's just some big jerk shoving you into a locker, who's gonna see?

Ryan Clancy

10 Julia [Reingold, one of Brendan's seventh-grade teachers] is a close friend and has amazing radar for the kids who are going to need support but might otherwise fall through the cracks. One of the kids she mentioned was Brendan, so I made sure he was one
15 of mine. I got him into my office one day, and he just about "yes, ma'amed" and "no, ma'amed" me to death. "Yes, ma'am, everything's fine." "No, ma'am, I don't have a problem with anyone." But you could

---

"'Every day being teased and picked on, pushed up against lock-
20 ers – just the general feeling of fear in the school. And you either respond to a fear by having fear, or you take action and have hate.'"

Brooks Brown, a student at Columbine High who knew both Eric Harris and Dylan Klebold, *Rolling Stone*, 6/10/99

---

5 f. **all-out:** aufs Ganze.   6 **knock-down-drag-out fight:** etwa: lange, heftige Prügelei.   7 **jerk:** Penner, Wichser.   8 **to shove:** schubsen. 13 **to fall through the cracks:** (fig.) durch die Maschen schlüpfen, unbeachtet bleiben.

see the pain and anger in his eyes. Of course, I had
fifty boys and girls like that, all of them feeling more
or less the same thing. And I was responsible for another 350, so what could I do?

5   *Beth Bender, Middletown High School counselor*

Brendan was starting to get known as someone who
refused to toe the line. He wouldn't bow down to the
football players. It was the fall, so in gym we were
playing flag football. Usually we just went outside and
10 messed around. There'd be two games: the "winner-
athlete" game and the "loser-geek" game. That day
Herr Bosco decided to show us losers the "right" way
to cover a pass receiver. The thing is we were only
playing flag football, just a bunch of dorks in T-shirts
15 and shorts.

    Bosco picked Sam Flach and Brendan to demonstrate.
Now, you knew right away that this was no accident.
Bosco hated Brendan's "attitude." So he said, "Sam

Several news organizations pointed out that the ratio of students
20 to counselors at Kipland Kinkel's high school was roughly 700
to 1.

---

5 **counselor:** Beratungslehrer(in), Vertrauenslehrer(in).   7 **to toe the
line:** sich einfügen.   **to bow down to s.o.:** sich jdm. unterwerfen, beugen.   9 **flag football:** Variante des American Football (ohne Schutz-
bekleidung und starken Körpereinsatz).   11 **loser-geek:** Loser-Typ.
12 **Herr:** hier: der Weißhaarige, Alte (von *hoary* ›ergraut‹).   13 **to
cover s.o.:** jdn. decken.   **pass:** Pass (American Football).   14 **dork:**
etwa: Idiot, Trottel.
[Subtext]   19 **ratio:** Verhältnis, Anteil.

and Lawlor, front and center." Jocks have first names. The rest of us mutants are last name only.

So I figure, maybe Sam's built like a brick outhouse, but Brendan's thin and fast, and I bet he'll try to beat
5 him off the line and get free. Like, welcome to Ryan's private little football fantasy, folks. Our big chance to surprise the jocks and show them that geeks can play in the big time.

Brendan sets up on the imaginary line of scrimmage,
10 and Sam's facing him five yards away with this smirk on his face. Like, *Come on, loser, show me what you've got.* And I'm dumb enough to be rooting for Brendan. Like, *This ain't the hall, Flach. There's room to move.*

Herr Bosco's the QB, and he yells, "Go!" Brendan
15 takes three steps, fakes left, goes right, and *POW!* Sam

"Like most students, I lived in fear of the small slights and public humiliations used to reinforce the rigid high school caste system: Poor girls were sluts, soft boys were fags. And at each of my schools, there were students who lived in daily fear of physical
20 violence."

A posting on the Internet after Columbine

---

2 **mutant:** Mutant, Abartige(r).   3 **to be built like a brick outhouse:** etwa: ein Kreuz wie ein Kleiderschrank haben.   5 **off the line:** (aus der Grundaufstellung) mit dem Ball 10 Yard Raumgewinn (in Richtung der gegnerischen Auslinie) (American Football).   **like:** so ungefähr.   6 **folks:** Leute.   9 **line of scrimmage:** Gedrängelinie.
10 **smirk:** süffisantes Grinsen.   13 **ain't** (infml.): *isn't*.   14 **QB:** Abk. für *Quarterback:* Mittelfeldspieler (American Football).   15 **to fake:** antäuschen.
[Subtext]   17 **humiliation:** Demütigung.   **to reinforce:** verstärken, bekräftigen.   18 **slut:** Schlampe.   **fag:** Schwuler.

knocks him right on his butt. You could see Brendan didn't know what hit him. He was flat on his back, probably seeing stars.

I look around, and all the jocks are sniggering and chuckling. And the biggest smirk is on Herr Bosco's face. "Uh, Sam," he goes, "this is flag football. No hitting."

Sam just smiles back. "Gee, sorry, Coach."

You could see that Brendan was still woozy as he got to his feet. You think Bosco bothers to ask if he's okay? No, he's too busy looking for the next victim. By then I'd backed away to the rear of the crowd, where all the geeks were cowering in fear, praying Herr Bosco wouldn't pick them next.

Ryan Clancy

Sam Flach will die slowly. I will shoot him in one knee, then the other, then a gut shot so he'll have no friggin' doubt where he's going. And he will stare up at me with a fear in his eyes he has never known, and I will put that friggin' barrel right against his forehead and say, "Gee, sorry, Sam," then blow his friggin' brains out.

An E-mail from Brendan to Gary

To be on the outside and watch it was amazing. Except the real word for it is probably more like *horrifying*. At the red-hot core were most of the football

---

1 **butt:** Hintern.　4 **to snigger:** kichern.　5 **to chuckle:** sich (leise) eins lachen.　8 **gee:** Mann!, oje!　9 **woozy:** benommen.　13 **to cower:** sich ducken.　17 **gut shot:** Bauchschuss.　25 **red-hot core:** innerster Kern, Zentrum.

players and some of the guys from the other teams, and the cheerleaders and some of the pretty girls. Ninety percent blondes, in case you haven't noticed.

Next came the rest of the athletes and a few popular
5 designer label guys who weren't athletes but were just really nice and likable, and the nicer girls and some of the pretty girls who were also popular and athletic. And then came the rest of us, only it didn't matter who or what we were. And that wasn't only the way we out-
10 siders saw it. It was the way everyone saw it. I mean, the teachers and the administrators. You'd get to class late, and they'd make you go back and get a pass. But Sam Flach would stroll in late and say he'd been talking to Coach Bosco, and that was just fine. Even the grown-
15 ups outside school, like the guy who pumped gas at the station and the lady who worked behind the counter at Starbucks. They all knew the football players by name,

---

"Outcasts loathed Columbine. With equal venom, they detested popular kids and an administration that in their minds kowtowed
20 to the popular kids."

Rolling Stone, 6/10/99

---

5 **designer label guy:** Typ in Designerklamotten.   11 **administrator:** (nicht unterrichtender) Angestellter der Schulverwaltung.   12 **to get a pass:** sich eine Entschuldigung holen.   13 **to stroll in:** hereinschlendern, hereinspaziert kommen.   15 **to pump gas:** Tankwart sein. 17 **Starbucks:** amerikanische Kette von Kaffeehäusern.
[Subtext]   18 **to loathe:** hassen, verabscheuen.   **venom:** Bosheit, Gehässigkeit.   **to detest:** verachten.   19f. **to kowtow to s.o.:** vor jdm. kriechen, einen Kotau machen, katzbuckeln.

and they'd do extra things for them, like wash their windshield or slip them a free brownie. There were days when you just felt like it was their world. And somehow you hadn't been picked to be part of it.

5   *Emily Kirsch*

Everyone around here knows the football players. Either they see them at the games or they read about them in the newspaper. From about the middle of August until the end of November the sports section is
10 all about the [Middletown] Marauders. And there'll be those human-interest stories in the other parts of the paper too. Like how Dustin Williams went to the elementary school to talk to the kids, or how Bosco got the team to spend a couple of hours cleaning up
15 some park so kids could play there. And there are always pictures of them, of course.

There's basketball and wrestling, too. Except the basketball team's not so hot, and even though the wrestling team is pretty good, the only people who
20 come watch them are the wrestlers' families and friends. The baseball team is like a joke, and you never even hear about the tennis and soccer teams. Then they cover stuff like girls' field hockey and volleyball just to be politically correct.

25 It's like, big stories and lots of photos about football, small stories and a few photos about basketball and

---

2 **to slip s.o. s.th.:** jdm. etwas zukommen lassen, zustecken. **brownie:** flacher Schokoladenkuchen.   10 **marauder:** Plünderer, Plünderin, Räuber(in).   11 **human-interest stories:** Geschichten über das Privatleben.   18 **hot:** toll, gut.

wrestling, and the rest is just box scores. You have to feel bad for the guys on the other teams. Unless they're total all-American superstars, they're not even noticed. And as far as the rest of us are concerned, the people in
5 this town don't even know we exist.

Ryan Clancy

Why shouldn't athletes be treated with more respect? They're the ones who are actually out there fighting for our school. Everybody thinks it's so great, but
10 how do you think it feels when they lose? Each one of those players has to feel responsible for that. Everyone else walks around saying, "Oh, we would have won if so-and-so hadn't dropped the ball." Meanwhile so-and-so has to come to school, and you
15 think he doesn't know what they're saying behind his back? How do you think that feels? I mean, being blamed. If [the athletes] have to take the blame for when they lose, shouldn't they get the rewards when they win? That's what school spirit is all about. The
20 fans aren't the ones who give our school its pride. It's the players. They're the ones that give Middletown a sense of accomplishment.

Deirdre Bunson

I love football. It's been a part of my life ever since I
25 was small. My parents have had season tickets for the Marauders for nearly forty years. I can count on one hand the number of Friday nights we've missed. Foot-

---

1 **box score:** Ergebnistabelle mit allen Punkten und den Namen aller Spieler.   3 **all-American:** national.   14 **so-and-so:** der So-und-So.
25 **season ticket:** Dauerkarte.

ball is part of the social fabric of this town. It brings
us together and gives us something to look forward to
and talk about. I firmly believe that it has a positive
and long-lasting benefit for the kids, and the adults as
5 well.

I love the excitement and the crowd and the food. I
love cheering for my students and the sons of my
friends. If a former student comes back to visit, I'm
more likely to see him or her at the game on Friday
10 night than anywhere else. I will be delighted if someday
my own son plays for the Marauders.

You cannot blame what happened here on football.
You simply have to think of the thousands of schools in
this country that have football teams, and where noth-
15 ing like this has ever happened. What happened here
goes much deeper.

Beth Bender

I think Brendan got it worse than the other kids. Like
you'd see a crowd of guys talking to some girls but in-
20 tentionally blocking the hall, you know? Like assert-
ing their power. Trying to impress the girls, or whatever. Some kids would see that and just, you know,
try to find another way around or wait until the crowd
broke up, even if it meant they'd be late. But Brendan
25 couldn't stand it. He knew what they were doing, and
it just made him nuts. Some jocks are saying that
Brendan went out of his way to start fights, but I

---

1 **social fabric:** Sozialstruktur.   19f. **intentionally** (adv.): absicht-
lich.   25 **to stand s.th.:** etwas aushalten.   26 **to make s.o. nuts:** jdn.
auf die Palme bringen.   27 **to go out of one's way to do s.th.:** einen
Grund suchen, etwas zu tun.

44

don't think it was that. I think he just felt really
strongly that he had a right to go down the hall and
that it was wrong for those guys to block it just to
prove they owned the place.

5   *Dustin Williams*

The chicken!&# teachers know what's going on. Today
friggin' Flach shoved me in the hall and called me a faggot right in front of Mr. Ellin. You know that jerk Ellin?
He's a new biology teacher. I think this is his first year.*
10 *He's one of those preppies in Gap chinos and a blue button-down shirt. Halfway between student and teacher.*
  *So he tells me I shouldn't take it personally. Can you
friggin' believe it? I get slammed and dissed, and I'm not*

"How many kids ostracized, humiliated, and assaulted in Ameri-
15 can high schools, like the survivors of Columbine High, are left
scarred for life? How many commit suicide every year? So long as
some kids go out of their way to make high school hell for others,
there are going to be kids who crack, and not all of the kids who
crack are going to quietly off themselves."

20   A posting on the Internet

---

6 **chicken:** feige.   **!&*# teacher:** Gemeint ist *fucking teacher:* Scheiß-
lehrer.   7 f. **faggot:** Schwuchtel, Schwule(r).   10 **preppy:** etwa: Yup-
pie, schnieker Typ, Popper.   **Gap chinos** (pl.): Marken-Jeans (*Gap:*
bekannter amerikanischer Textilhersteller).   10 f. **button-down shirt:**
Hemd mit Kragenknöpfen.   11 **halfway:** (auf dem halben Weg)
zwischen.   13 **to get slammed:** eine geknallt kriegen.   **to get dissed:**
heruntergeputzt, fertig gemacht werden.
[Subtext]   14 **to ostracize s.o.:** jdn. schneiden, ausschließen.   **to hu-
miliate s.o.:** jdn. demütigen.   15 **survivor:** Überlebende(r).   16 **scarred for life:** fürs Leben gezeichnet.   **to commit suicide:** Selbstmord
begehen.   18 **to crack:** (psychisch) zerbrechen.

supposed to take it personally? I mean, why didn't he
drag Flach's butt down to [Principal] Curry's office?

These stupid teachers, you know? Especially the new,
young ones. They think they're like you. Like you've got
5 something in common. Like I'd ever want to be a friggin'
teacher.

So, you'll love this. Ellin tells me it's all genetics. The
athletes are the dominant males, and they're driven by
their friggin' genes to keep the rest of the pack in line.
10 Like the next time one of them smashes my face into the
friggin' lockers, I'm supposed to forgive him because he's
not really doin' it, it's his friggin' genes making him do it.

I mean, who gives a rat's ass why they do it? What the
hell difference does it make? You think some loser getting
15 his butt whipped really gives a flying #$*% whether the
guy who's doing it personally hates his guts or is just
being driven by some friggin' chromosome? Gimme a
break. When I take 'em out, I'm gonna make sure I nail
this guy Ellin just because he tried to give it a reason.
20 Like an excuse or something. Like he thinks maybe on

More than 50 percent of male youths say it would be easy to obtain a gun.

---

7 **genetics** (pl.): Genetik, Vererbungslehre.   8 **dominant male:** domi-
nantes Männchen.   9 **to keep s.o. in line:** jdn. nicht aus der Reihe
tanzen lassen.   **pack:** Meute.   13 **to give a rat's ass:** sich einen
Dreck kümmern.   15 **to give a flying #$*%:** sich einen Scheiß küm-
mern.   16 **to hate s.o.'s guts:** jdn. auf den Tod nicht ausstehen können.   17 **chromosome:** Chromosom (Erbgut tragendes Gebilde im
Zellkern).   **gimme** (infml.): *give me.*   18 **to take s.o. out:** jdn. alle
machen, beseitigen.   **to nail s.o.:** sich jdn. schnappen.

*some level that makes it understandable. If that's under-
standable, so's popping a cap in his ass with a friggin' TEC-9.*

An E-mail from Brendan to Gary

The boys call each other a few names, and in no time,
unless one of them backs down, they're fighting. It's
different with girls. It's all backbiting and nastiness.
The popular girls wouldn't dream of fighting. They
might chip a nail. They fight with words and looks
and searing little offhand comments designed to cut
your heart out. Everyone wants to be young again,
but each time I see these girls reduce someone to
tears, it makes me think twice.

Beth Bender

Maybe we stereotype them, but they stereotype us,
too. To them we're all big dumb jocks. They seem to
forget that Dustin Williams's GPA is way up there,
and so are a couple of other guys'. And who says they
don't want to be stereotyped? If you walk around this
school putting it down and dissing on sports and
spirit, aren't you kind of just asking to be stereotyped?

Paul Burns, football player

2 **to pop a cap:** eine Patrone ballern.   **TEC-9:** halbautomatische
9-mm-Pistole des Herstellers Illinois Firearm Resource.   6 **to back-
bite:** lästern.   **nastiness:** Bosheit.   8 **to chip a nail:** (sich) einen (Fin-
ger-)Nagel abbrechen.   9 **searing:** schneidend, gemein.   **offhand:**
spontan; lässig.   9 f. **to cut s.o.'s heart out:** jdn. bis ins Herz treffen.
11 f. **to reduce s.o. to tears:** jdn. zum Weinen bringen.   14 **to stereotype:** klischeehaft darstellen.   16 **GPA:** Abk. für *grade point average:*
Notendurchschnitt.   19 **to put s.th. down:** etwas runtermachen.

You're walking down the hall, minding your own business. You see this guy, and he just sneers at you and says, "Hey, faggot." Thing is, to him it's nothing. Two seconds later he's probably forgotten he even
5 said it. But it's burned in your brain. It's a permanent scar. A week later you're still asking yourself, why'd he have to do that? Why'd he have to pick you? Does everyone think you're a faggot? Maybe you are a faggot and you don't even know it.

10 It's like torture. You know "Sticks and stones will break my bones, but names will never hurt me"? It's a load of crap. A stick stops hurting after a few minutes. Names last a long time.

Ryan Clancy

15 I was talking with Brendan in the hall, and Sam Flach came by and gave him just the slightest nudge. The sort of harmless thing that must happen a thousand times a day in a crowded school like ours. At first I thought Brendan overreacted. Making a fist, mutter-
20 ing under his breath. I stupidly said, "Oh, come on,

"I went to three [high schools], and in none of [them] did I for a moment feel safe. High school was terrifying, and it was the casual cruelty of the popular kids that made it hell."

A posting on the Internet

---

1 f. **to mind one's own business:** sich um seine eigenen Angelegenheiten kümmern.   2 **to sneer at s.o.:** jdn. höhnisch angrinsen.   12 **load of crap:** Haufen Scheiße.   16 **nudge:** Knuff, leichter Stoß.   19 f. **to mutter:** murmeln.   20 **under one's breath:** leise vor sich hin. [Subtext]   22 **terrifying:** schrecklich, entsetzlich.   22 f. **casual:** beiläufig.

Brendan, it wasn't that bad, just a little push." Brendan looked back at me with such hurt in his eyes. He said, "No, Ms. Bender, it's not 'just' a little push, not when it happens every day." Even then I didn't take it
5 that seriously. But now I think I understand. What if it really was constant, unrelenting torment? A little bit of salt doesn't bother your skin. But that same small amount in an open wound can really, really sting.
10   *Beth Bender*

It wasn't just in the halls. It was everywhere. Once, in gym, we were out in the field a couple of days after a big rain. The grass had pretty much dried, but there were still a few puddles. Next thing I know, [Sam]
15 Flach and [Paul] Burns push me down. Each one grabs a leg, and they drag me through a couple of muddy puddles. I'm drenched with grimy water and smeared with mud, and Bosco comes over, and I swear he's having a really hard time not grinning. He
20 tells Flach and Burns to let go and tells me to go clean up. And that was it. I mean, it was almost like he was giving those guys a license to do it again anytime they liked.
                                           Ryan Clancy

25 Everyone thinks about suicide when they're a teenager. At least, almost everyone I know. It's just, like,

---

6 **unrelenting:** unnachgiebig, unerbittlich.   **torment:** Quälerei.
14 **puddle:** Pfütze.   17 **to be drenched:** klatschnass sein.   **grimy:** verdreckt.   18 **smeared:** beschmiert.

something really crappy happens and you're in this horrible pain, and what's the point? Gary loved that old Queen song, the one they sang in the car in *Wayne's World*. You know, where the singer says he
5 shot someone in the head and his life is ruined, but nothing really matters anyway. I mean, don't take this the wrong way and think you've made some big discovery. He didn't do what he did because of some stupid song.
10 *Allison Findley*

Lots of kids'll say they want to kill themselves at one point or another, but Gary would really go into detail about it. I remember he once got into this whole thing about hanging himself from the flagpole in front of
15 the school. So you'd get to school the next morning, and instead of the flag, there'd be Gary. The thing of it was he couldn't figure out how to do it. Like, how would he get up there? He thought maybe a really long extension ladder would do the trick. I figured it
20 was just typical Gary stuff, but a couple of days later we were leaving school, and he actually took off his

---

The presence of a gun in the home increases the risk of suicide fivefold.

---

1 **something crappy:** etwas Beschissenes.   3 **Queen:** britische Rockband der siebziger und achtziger Jahre um den Sänger Freddie Mercury; gemeint ist das Lied »Bohemian Rhapsody«.   4 **"Wayne's World":** Filmkomödie aus dem Jahr 1992 über zwei Jugendliche mit einer eigenen Fernsehshow.   14 **flagpole:** Fahnenmast.   19 **extension ladder:** Ausziehleiter.
[Subtext]   23 **fivefold:** um das Fünffache.

backpack and tried to shimmy up the flagpole. Of course he couldn't. But it really hit me: Two days later and he's still thinking about it.

Ryan Clancy

5 I can't begin to count how many times on a Saturday around noon I'd knock on Gary's door and find him still in bed, wide awake, simply lying there with that thick quilt wrapped around him like a cocoon. I'd suggest that he go outside, find someone to do some-
10 thing with. He'd always say he would "in a moment." But sometimes he wouldn't get out of bed until three or four. I always felt as if there was something inside keeping him from being happy and active like other boys. A lead curtain of sadness that was too heavy for
15 him to lift. I'm sure it had to do with the divorce. I can't tell you how many times I'd see him like that, then go into my own room and just cry.

Cynthia Searle

"Most of the attackers in the recent cases had shown signs of
20 clinical depression or other psychological problems. But schools, strapped for mental health counselors, are less likely to pick up on such behavior or to have the available help."

New York Times, 6/14/98

---

1 **backpack:** Rucksack. **to shimmy up:** sich hoch schieben, hoch klettern. 8 **quilt:** Steppdecke; Federbett. **cocoon:** Kokon, Hülle. 14 **lead:** bleiern.
[Subtext] 21 (*to be*) **strapped for s.th.:** Mangel an etwas haben. 21 f. **to pick up on s.th.:** sich um etwas kümmern.

This one night I came home pretty late. It was definitely after midnight. Brendan was sitting in the dark on the curb in front of his house. Elbows on his knees, his head hung. Looking pretty bummed. So I went
5 over and asked if everything was okay. He said no as if it was obvious things weren't okay. I guess it was a dumb question, so I apologized. He patted the curb next to him. You know, have a seat.

I sat down. You could smell the liquor on him, and
10 I think I might have said something about drinking alone. He got into this rap about how we were both minorities, him being an outcast and me being African American. And didn't I know that if it weren't for football, I'd be in the same boat as him? I told him I
15 thought there might be some truth to that, but that while there were definitely some bigots around, the majority of people we knew were smart enough to know better.

He asked if I knew that some of the worst bigots in
20 school were on the team. I said I didn't think that was the case. We talked a little more, and then I got up and said I had to get to bed. Practice the next day, you know? I asked if he was going in, and he shook his head

---

The number of kids killed by firearms has quadrupled in the past
25 ten years.

People, 5/3/99

---

3 **curb:** Bordstein. 4 **bummed:** fertig, deprimiert. 7 **to pat s.th.:**
auf etwas klopfen. 9 **liquor:** Alkohol. 11 **rap:** Gequatsche.
16 **bigot:** bigotter Typ, Frömmler(in).
[Subtext] 24 **firearm:** Schusswaffe. **to quadruple:** sich vervierfachen. 26 **"People":** amerikanische Tageszeitung.

and said he was going to stay out for a while more. He tried to be tough and cool, but right at that moment he looked mostly miserable and weak.

Since we'd been talking pretty intimately, I asked him why he was doing this to himself. You know, drinking alone and fighting and generally making himself an outsider. He just looked up at me. Maybe it was my imagination, but I thought his eyes were glistening, like with tears. And then he said that if I weren't on the team, I'd want to kill each and every one of them too. I said I was sorry but I didn't see it that way.

Dustin Williams

If you're going to teach ninth-grade English, you have to be prepared for some off-the-wall stuff, especially from a kid like Brendan Lawlor. You see kids like him every year. You get the feeling they're at war in their mind, fighting some constant battle inside themselves as well as with everyone around them. Brendan wrote poems that sounded like plots for nightmarish action movies. Poems about automatic-weapons fire, limbs being torn off, the smell of burning flesh, skulls crushed and brains splattered in the halls, bombs, people begging for mercy before having their throats slit, then blowing yourself away. You would almost assume it was satire, except that for a kid like Brendan it was deadly serious. There were times when you

---

4 **intimately** (adv.): vertraut.   8 **to glisten:** glitzern; nass werden.
14 **off-the-wall:** irre, verrückt.   19 **nightmarish:** alptraumartig.
22 **to splatter:** spritzen.   23f. **to have one's throat slit:** die Kehle durchgeschnitten bekommen.   24 **to blow o.s. away:** sich wegpusten, umbringen.

wanted to take him by the shoulders and shake him. *Come on, wake-up! You're young. You've got your whole life ahead of you. Buckle down, work hard, go on a date, go to college, and get on with it.*

5 *Dick Flanagan, Brendan's ninth-grade English teacher at Middletown High School*

---

3 **to buckle down:** sich dranmachen.   3f. **to go on a date:** sich verabreden.

Part of Brendan's Suicide Note

Know what? Not everybody has to do what you A-holes want them to do. Maybe your kids did, but me and my friends chose not to. And you and your kids couldn't deal
5 with that. And so you had to do what stupid, ignorant people always do when they don't understand – you had to attack and torment us.

And you teachers. I thought you taught us that America is supposed to be about freedom. Kids are supposed to be
10 able to be different without the status quo police smashing us over the head and ridiculing us. But that's all you teachers did to me and my friends. Just like everyone else, you tried to make us conform to your narrow-minded expectations of how we were supposed to dress
15 and act.

Well, screw you. Screw all of you. I hope this letter is like a knife in your hearts. You ruined my life. All I've done is pay you back in kind.

---

2 **A-hole:** *asshole, arsehole:* Arschloch. 7 **to torment:** quälen.
10 **status quo police:** Status-quo-Polizei; Polizei, die darauf besteht, dass das Bestehende nicht verändert wird. 11 **to ridicule:** sich lustig machen. 13 f. **narrow-minded:** engstirnig. 16 **screw you:** ihr könnt mich mal. 18 **to pay s.o. back in kind:** es jdm. mit gleicher Münze heimzahlen.

More of Ninth Grade

Gary thought it was all a big joke anyway. He always
said life was an accident. I mean, life on this planet. It
wasn't anything that was meant to be. Most of the
5 time I didn't bother to argue. But sometimes it made
me sad. People tell me I'm really angry inside. It's
probably true. But at least now I think maybe it can
get better. But to Gary it was always hopeless and
meaningless.
10   I think his mom might have been religious. Anyway,
I hear she's been going to church a lot since what happened.

Allison Findley

One day in class we were talking about morality, and
15 Brendan said there was no God. He didn't say that *he*
didn't believe in God. He just said there was no God.
Like he had this special knowledge and that was just
the way it was, take it or leave it. The whole class
went quiet. Even Mr. Flanagan was kind of shocked.
20 He said Brendan could feel that way if he wanted, but
that was his opinion and not necessarily the truth. But
Brendan, he just kept saying there was no God. Like
it wasn't enough to say what he believed. He had to

---

18 **take it or leave it:** ganz egal, was andere denken.

try and force it down everyone else's throat too. I really wanted to pound the crap out of him.

Paul Burns

It's stupid to point at one incident and say, "It's all
5 because of this." It has to be something that builds gradually and eats at you for a long time until you go psycho. But having said that, I'll tell you about one thing that happened in ninth grade that really changed Brendan. It was the time they did the swirly
10 to him. They held him by the ankles and dunked his head in the toilet. It was all over school in no time. After Gary and I heard about it, we went looking for [Brendan], but he was gone.

Ryan Clancy

15 Face it, there are two sets of rules: one for those who are in favor and one for those who aren't. If Deirdre Bunson is talking in world history, it's like, "Excuse

---

Several people said immediately after the shooting that Michael Carneal was an atheist, or at least had associated with atheists.

---

1 **to force s.th. down s.o.'s throat:** jdm. etwas aufzwingen. 2 **to pound the crap out of s.o.:** jdm. diesen Scheiß rausprügeln. 6 **to eat at s.o.:** an jdm. nagen. 6f. **to go psycho:** verrückt werden, durchdrehen. 9f. **to do the swirly to s.o.:** jdn. mit dem Kopf ins Klo halten. 10 **to dunk:** (ein)tauchen, (ein)tunken. 11 **in no time:** in null Komma nichts, im Handumdrehen.
[Subtext] 19 **Carneal:** Der 14-jährige Michael C. tötete am 1.12. 1997 in der Heath High School, Paducah (Kentucky), drei Mädchen und verletzte fünf weitere Schüler. In seinem Rucksack fanden sich 500 Schuss Munition. Vgl. S. 170.

me, Deirdre, now pay attention." But if Allison Findley is talking, Ms. Arnold stops the class and stares at
her. And then the rest of the kids stare at her. It's a
light slap on the wrist for Deirdre. It's public humili-
5 ation for Allison.

Allison Findley

[Brendan] called me the second night. I said, "Brendan, where have you been [for the past two days]?"
He said he'd been ditching. He couldn't face anyone
10 at school. I asked why he didn't tell his parents or the
school, and he just laughed. He said if the guys who
did [the swirly] found out [he'd told on them], it
would only make it worse. He went to school the next
day and got two weeks' detention for unexplained ab-
15 sence. Is that fair?

Emily Kirsch

Everybody's looking for someone to blame. So, of
course, since I'm on the [football] team and I had
some scrapes with those guys, a lot of people want to
20 blame me. Let me tell you something. I'm not going
to deny that I mixed it up with them. I did it, and I'm
not proud of it. Obviously, after what they did to me,
I'm gonna regret it for as long as I live. But there's
just one thing. It wasn't like I went looking for them.
25 Those guys, especially Brendan, it was like he always

---

4 **slap:** Klaps. **wrist:** Handgelenk 9 **to ditch:** blaumachen. 12 **to
tell on s.o.:** jdn. verpetzen. 14 **detention:** Nachsitzen. 14f. **unexplained absence:** unentschuldigtes Fehlen. 19 **scrapes:** Schwierigkeiten,
Probleme. 21 **to mix it up with s.o.:** sich mit jdm. anlegen, zanken,
Streit mit jdm. suchen.

wanted to start something. Like he went out of his
way to ask for it.

Sam Flach

Like all other animals, we are born with instincts and
a genetic blueprint of what we must do to survive.
The big difference is that humans possess the poten-
tial for becoming civilized, thinking, *reasoning* crea-
tures. Eventually we are supposed to learn to sup-
press our animal instincts in order to meld with the
society around us.

But at what point is the process of suppressing our
animal instincts complete? Seven years of age? Fourteen? Twenty-one? In other words, do we expect too
much of teenagers?

F. Douglas Ellin, a biology teacher at Middletown
High School

I suppose I'm as much at fault as anyone. But it's not
like football players are monsters. Kids have been

In 1995 alone, 35,957 Americans were killed by firearms in
homicides, suicides, and accidents. In comparison, during the
three years of the Korean War, 33,651 Americans were killed.
During nearly eight years of the war in Vietnam, 58,148 Americans were killed.

---

5 **blueprint:** Blaupause, Plan.   9 **to meld:** sich (ver)mischen.   17 **to
be at fault:** schuld sein, Schuld haben.
[Subtext]   20 **homicide:** Tötungsdelikt.   21 **Korean War:** Korea-
krieg (von 1950 bis 1953; endete mit der Teilung des Landes).
22 **war in Vietnam:** Vietnamkrieg (von 1955 bis 1975; endete mit dem
Rückzug der USA und der Wiedervereinigung des Landes unter kom-
munistischer Herrschaft).

getting into fights and picking on one another since forever. I don't know why Brendan and Gary did what they decided to do, but to say it was all because some football players picked on them has to be a
5 gross oversimplification.

Dustin Williams

There is an unwritten law here about the treatment of athletes, especially those athletes on the teams that have a chance to go to the playoffs and bring the
10 school recognition and enhance its pride. In our case, that's football and wrestling. The [unwritten] law states that you may discipline a student athlete up to a point. But it must be an absolutely extraordinary situation for you to do anything that would impinge
15 on that athlete's ability to play for his team. To do so would be to invite the worst kind of scorn, not just from the football coaches, but from the administration, other teachers, and the town at large. Do a few of the athletes know this and take advantage of
20 it? What do you think?

Beth Bender

With the trend toward two parents working and spending less time at home, the responsibility for raising children and instilling them with values rests
25 more and more on the shoulders of the schools. We

---

5 **oversimplification:** übertriebene Vereinfachung. 9 **playoff:** Entscheidungsspiel. 10 **to enhance:** steigern. 12 **to discipline:** disziplinieren. 14 f. **to impinge on s.th.:** sich auf etwas auswirken. 16 **scorn:** Verachtung. 18 **at large** (adv.): allgemein. 24 **to instill s.o. with s.th.:** (fig.) jdm. etwas einflößen.

are no longer supposed to teach just academics; we are now supposed to rear, nurture, coddle, protect, encourage, discipline, and teach good hygiene and eating habits. If you're a teacher with six classes of roughly thirty kids each, how exactly are you supposed to do that?

Allen Curry, principal of Middletown High School

My mother says I'm a pack rat. I save everything. I don't know why, I just do. Gary, Brendan, Allison, and I would get into a chat room and shoot the breeze, and if I thought it was interesting, I'd save it onto a Zip drive. As soon as the cops found out, they got a warrant and came in here and took it all away, but my dad went to court and got some of it back after the cops made copies. After what happened, I went back and started to look at some of the stuff. I thought this one was pretty interesting. Brendan is TerminX. Gary is Dayzd. Allison is Blkchokr, and I'm Rebooto.

Ryan Clancy

---

2 **to nurture:** aufziehen, fördern.   **to coddle:** umhegen, verhätscheln.   8 **pack rat:** Buschschwanzratte (sammelt Gegenstände in ihrem Nest).   10 **to shoot the breeze:** einfach rumalbern.   12 **Zip drive:** Zip-Laufwerk.   **cop:** Bulle, Polizist.   13 **warrant:** Durchsuchungsbefehl.   18 **TerminX:** *terminator:* Vollstrecker; vermutl. abgeleitet von dem zweiten Teil des Films *Terminator* (1984) mit dem Titel *Judgment Day* aus dem Jahr 1991 mit Arnold Schwarzenegger in der Hauptrolle.   **Dayzd:** *dazed:* verwirrt; mögliche Anspielung auf den Film *Dazed and Confused* aus dem Jahr 1993 über den letzten Schultag von Highschool-Schülern.   **Blkchokr:** *black choker:* schwarzer Halsreif.   19 **Rebooto:** Wortspiel mit *to reboot* ›(Computer) neu laden‹ und *ReBoot*, einer TV-Serie 1994–2001 über Computer(spiele).

TerminX: *Burns called me a nerd 2day.*

Blkchokr: *Feeble*

Rebooto: *That's the best he could come up with!*

Dayzd: *Know what he'll call a nerd 10 years from now?*

5 **TerminX:** *Boss*

Rebooto: *LOL!*

TerminX: *It's BS.*

Blkchokr: *Y?*

TerminX: *Jocks go 2 college and play on teams. They're*
10 *heroes.*

Rebooto: *They get hot babes.*

Dayzd: *They get babes hot.*

TerminX: *They study accounting and pre-law. Then they*
screw up their knees and their career is over. But it
15 *doesn't matter.*

Blkchokr: *Y not?*

TerminX: *Because they're still winners.*

Dayzd: *We're losers, with good knees.*

Rebooto: *Unless U lose Ur knee.*

20 **Dayzd:** *Or Ur knee comes loose.*

TerminX: *They become partners in accounting firms and*
law firms, and everyone wants 2 work with them because
they were heroes in college.

Blkchokr: *Some go into pro sports.*

---

1 **nerd:** Computerfreak; Schwachkopf. **2day:** *today*. 2 **feeble:** schwach. 6 **LOL:** Abk. für *laughing out loud.* 7 **BS:** Abk. für *bullshit:* Quatsch, Mist. 8 **Y:** *why.* 9 **2:** *to.* 13 **accounting:** Buchführung. **pre-law:** Vorbereitungskurs fürs Jurastudium. 14 **to screw up one's knees:** sich die Knie kaputtmachen. 19 **U:** *you.* **Ur:** *your.* 21 **accounting firm:** Buchprüfungsfirma. 22 **law firm:** Anwaltskanzlei. 24 **pro:** hier: Profi-.

TerminX: *It's incredibly rare.*
Dayzd: *About as rare as some nerd actually being Ur boss.*

---

1 **incredibly** (adv.): unglaublich.

Part of Gary's Suicide Note

Mom, I could never tell you how unhappy I was. I knew there was nothing you could do to help, and life has been hard enough on you already. I'm truly, truly sorry that I'm going to put you through so much pain, but I hope that in a year or two you'll get over it. Maybe you could move away and change your name and even have a new kid.

You can start over. I wish I could be there with you, but I'm past the point of no return.

---

8 **to start over:** neu anfangen.   9 **point of no return:** Punkt, an dem es kein Zurück mehr gibt.

The End of Ninth Grade

We talked all the time about getting back at the jocks.
For every time they called you a faggot. For every
time they bodychecked you into a wall. And every
5 teacher who saw it happen day after day and never
did anything more than tell those morons to stop
horsing around. We would tie them up and use pliers
to pull their fingernails off. We would gouge their
eyes out and castrate them. We would burn their
10 noses off with propane torches. I know it must sound
sick, but that's how pissed we were. You had these
guys breaking the rules and beating on you, and no
one tried to stop them.

Ryan Clancy

15 Brendan learned I had weapons in the house, because
he saw me carrying the case to the car one day when I
went [to a gun show]. A few days later he came over
and asked about them. I opened the case and let him

According to federal estimates, there are about 280 million
20 people and 240 million guns in America.

---

4 **to bodycheck:** rempeln. 6 **moron:** Schwachsinnige(r). 7 **to horse
around:** herumalbern. **pliers** (pl.): Zange. 8 f. **to gouge out:** aus-
stechen. 9 **to castrate:** kastrieren. 10 **propane torch:** Schweiß-
brenner.

hold a few. He was certainly surprised at how heavy some of them were. I think he said something to the tune of "I can't believe they're real."

Jack Phillips, a neighbor of Brendan's

5 *I will kill every friggin' one of them. It's gonna be Colum-*
bine all over again, only better. Harris and Klebold did it
right. Blow the friggin' school, then blow yourself away. I
wish I could have met them. Maybe we'll go under-
ground after Middletown. Help other outcasts kill the
10 *A-hole jocks at their schools. Or die trying. This is the*
new revolution. This is John Friggin' Brown telling the
country we've had enough of this crap. This is one for the
history books. Keep fighting until they bring you down in
a hail of bullets. Mark my words, Littleton was just the
15 *beginning.*

An E-mail from Brendan to Gary

The first gun Brendan got he bought from this kid in school. The thing is, if you know anything about this

---

Virtually all of the semiautomatic pistols manufactured in Brazil
20 are exported because Brazilian law forbids civilian ownership of
such guns.

Making a Killing

2f. **to the tune of:** etwa wie … . 8f. **to go underground:** in den Untergrund gehen, abtauchen. 11 **John Brown:** militanter Gegner der Sklaverei, der 1859 nach einem Überfall auf eine Waffenfabrik in Harpers Ferry (West Virginia) gefangen, vor Gericht gestellt und gehängt wurde. 14 **hail:** Hagel.
[Subtext] 19 **virtually** (adv.): so gut wie. **semiautomatic:** halbautomatisch. 20 **civilian ownership:** Privatbesitz. 21 **"Making a Killing":** Buchveröffentlichung von 1999; vgl. S. 174 (*to make a killing:* einen Reibach machen).

stuff, [the gun he bought] was a piece of crap. I think
it was made in Brazil or someplace. Brendan said he
paid a hundred [dollars] for it, and I heard someone
say that the kid who sold it to him had bought it for,
5 like, thirty. But Brendan didn't care. All he cared
about was having that gun.

Ryan Clancy

Brendan was changing. Definitely getting darker and
angrier, although sometimes he'd be the old Bren-
10 dan, funny and charming and goofy. It was probably
about a month after they did the swirly on him when
he called up and said he wanted to go up to the park.
Usually we'd just sit under a tree near the parking lot
and talk and drink, but this time there was someplace
15 he really wanted to get to. You could tell there was
something on his mind. We got into the park, and he
was like, "Let's go up on the hill." It's a big hill, and
Gary and I were really huffing and puffing. I have to
quit smoking. We got up there, and he took this gun
20 out of his pocket. Like, first we thought it was a toy,
then Gary thought maybe a starter's pistol. Brendan
said it was real, and I asked what he was going to do
with it. I won't use the words he used, but basically
he said he was going to blow away some kids at
25 school.

Allison Findley

10 **goofy:** dösig.   13 **parking lot:** Parkplatz.   16f. **he was like:** er ungefähr so.   18 **to huff and puff:** schnaufen und keuchen.   23 **basically** (adv.): im Grunde, eigentlich.

My dad has a 9 mm Glock he keeps on a shelf in his
bedroom closet. It's got that nice black finish like the
ones you see on TV. When we used to go on camping
trips, he'd put it in the glove compartment of our car.
5 The thing is I know some kids who really have ar-
senals – like rifles, shotguns, and pistols. I'm not talking about their fathers. I'm talking about them. Although their fathers have lots of guns too. So when
Brendan showed me this gun he'd bought, I was
10 pretty much, are you for real? I think he thought I
was surprised he had a gun, but I was like, "Give me
a break, that's not a gun, it's a toy." Man, I wish I
hadn't said that.

Ryan Clancy

15 Have you ever noticed how the staff wear their
walkie-talkies on their hip? I know that's the logical
place for them, but I can't help thinking of the simi-
larity to the sheriff and his deputies in the Wild West.
The way they're so quick to point that walkie-talkie at
20 kids who are misbehaving. As if it's loaded with com-
munication bullets. *If you don't respect my authority,
I'll call in the reinforcements.* When I was in school,

Among students who said they carried a gun, 53 percent said they
had obtained the gun from home or family; 37 percent obtained
25 the gun "off the street."

---

1 **Glock:** amerikanischer Schusswaffenhersteller.   2 **closet:** Wand-
schrank.   4 **glove compartment:** Handschuhfach.   6 **shotgun:**
Schrotflinte.   11 f. **give me a break:** mach mal halblang.   16 **walkie-
talkie:** Sprechfunkgerät.   20 **to misbehave:** sich schlecht beneh-
men.   22 **reinforcement:** Verstärkung.

the principal didn't carry a walkie-talkie. He didn't
need one. We respected his authority. Or we feared it.
You can say the staff need their walkie-talkies because there's no respect for authority anymore. But
5 perhaps there would be respect if the staff weren't so
quick to rely on threats. I don't know. Anyway, it
probably doesn't even matter. It's probably too late
now to change.

Beth Bender

10 [Brendan] was very interested, very respectful. He
wouldn't touch a gun unless he asked first. But he was
fascinated by them. He had to pick up each one, get
the feel of it, sight it. You know, the very same things
gun people do. He was a natural.

Jack Phillips
15

Gary asked me if I would get him a gun. He'd prepared his argument very carefully. Lots of kids had
guns. He'd take a safety course. It was for target practice only. I said I didn't believe in having guns. As far
20 as I was concerned, there was no place in our home

"Mitchell Johnson's mother … said … that she taught her boy
how to shoot a shotgun, and then he took a three-week course."

New York Times, 6/14/98

---

13 **to sight:** durchs Visier (einer Schusswaffe) sehen.   14 **natural:**
Naturtalent.   18 f. **target practice:** Zielübung.
[Subtext]   21 **Johnson:** Am 24. 3. 1998 erschossen der 11-jährige An-
drew Golden und der 13-jährige Mitchell J. in der Westside Middle
School, Jonesboro (Arkansas), vier Schüler und einen Lehrer und ver-
letzten zehn weitere Personen. Vgl. S. 170.

for one. I'd be lying if I said it didn't cross my mind
that he might use it on himself.

Cynthia Searle

You know how sometimes you go to a movie and you
5 come out and for a little while you sort of feel like one
of the characters? Maybe you even talk like them?
Brendan, Gary, and I went to one of these dumb horror movies. There's a scene where the killer guy picks
up one of his victims and throws him off an overpass,
10 right in front of a big truck going underneath.
   So, it's night and we were walking home, and Brendan stops on the overpass and watches the cars going
by underneath. He just stood there. Gary and I called
to him to come on, but he wouldn't. We didn't know
15 what he was doing. All of a sudden he starts to throw
something. It turned out he wasn't throwing anything,
just going through the motion. But it looked like it to
us, and to the cars underneath. There's this horrible
screeching and squealing of tires, and you knew cars
20 were skidding and swerving to get out of the way, and
you're sure any second you're going to hear a crash, but
it didn't happen.
   I wanted to run, get out of there before someone
came up and caught us. But Brendan wouldn't run.
25 He just walked up to us with a big smile on his face
and said, didn't we think that was the wicked coolest
thing?

Allison Findley

9 **overpass:** (Straßen-)Überführung.   17 **to go through the motion:**
(nur) die Bewegung machen.   19 **to screech:** kreischen.   **to squeal:**
quietschen.   20 **to skid:** rutschen.   **to swerve:** schleudern.

Whatever that dark thing in Brendan was, it started to come out in Gary, too. I always thought of Gary as more lost and sad than angry. I mean, I don't know whether what Gary had came from Brendan, or whether Brendan just brought it out in Gary. I hate to say this, but maybe it would have come out in Gary even if Brendan hadn't been there. But the two of them together ... I don't know, they just fed off each other.

Emily Kirsch

Allison [Findley] worried me too. She came to school in dirty clothes, with dirty hair, and sometimes, to be blunt, she smelled. I was concerned for her, both because I wondered if there was something wrong at home, and because of the way the other girls treated her. She was a bit overweight, but also very well developed. You would hear things. I had no way of knowing if they were true. I hoped they weren't.

Beth Bender

We hear all the time about the supposed deterioration of the behavior of young people over the past thirty years. Can we really put a value judgment on it? Maybe the behavior of teenagers has changed, but I'm not sure that implies deterioration. We read that with parents working so much and grandparents off in their retirement villages, there are far fewer adults

---

8 f. **to feed off each other:** sich gegenseitig anstacheln.   20 f. **deterioration:** Verschlechterung.   22 f. **to put s.th. on s.th. else:** etwas mit einer anderen Sache belegen.   26 **retirement village:** Wohnsiedlung für Rentner.

around to influence youngsters. The articles do make one interesting point – that in the absence of real adult role models, violent television and video images have become the substitute role models. I think that's
5 probably true.

F. Douglas Ellin

At the request of the police, Dick Flanagan and I went back and collected some of [Gary's and Brendan's] writings. We were both struck by how certain
10 themes came out, not necessarily in any one piece of writing, but in the body of work as a whole. It was clear that Gary felt weak and defenseless. He wrote often about characters who were teased and picked on. The themes in Brendan's writings were less clear
15 but much more aggressive. More like you were in some extremely violent video game. The characters in his stories were always getting revenge, always on the attack with weapons capable of terrible destruction.

Allen Curry

20 Brendan was seriously into [first-person shooter video games]. If you want to know the truth, so were a lot of other kids who didn't do what he did. But one day Gary and I are in his room with him, just hacking around on the computer and listening to music, and
25 Brendan's like, "Point and click, point and click!" Like he's just figured something out, you know? So he goes crawling into his closet and comes out with

---

20 f. **first-person shooter video game:** gewalttätiges Videospiel, bei dem es darum geht, den Partner zu töten.   23 f. **to hack around:** rumhacken.

that crappy little gun, and he aims it at me. I guess he saw the look on my face, because he said, "Don't worry, it's not loaded." Then he dry-fires the [gun] and it goes *click*, and he says, "See? Point and click! It's the same thing!"

Ryan Clancy

No one is naive enough to believe that violent movies or television or video games *can actually make* anyone commit a violent act. The real question is, If someone is inclined toward violence, do these forms of media help show him the way to do it?

F. Douglas Ellin

Brendan got into this "point and click" thing for a while. At lunch he'd put his arm on the table and plant his chin behind it so it looked like he was peeking over a wall. Then he'd stick his thumb up and point his finger at the kids he hated. He'd go, "Point and click, point and click. Die suckas." Like he was picking them off one by one.

Allison Findley

This one was after that school shooting in Idaho.

Ryan Clancy

The average twelve-year-old has seen more than seven thousand murders on television.

---

3 **to dry-fire:** (ohne Munition) abdrücken.   15f. **to peek:** schauen, spähen, lugen.   18 **suckas:** *suckers:* Schweine, Lutscher.

TerminX: *Gun control is friggin' stupid. Gunz don't kill people. People kill people.*
Rebooto: *But if people can't get gunz …*
TerminX: *They find a way.*
5 **Dayzd:** *My granddad's from WY. Everyone has gunz. U get a .22 at 10 and hunt squirrels.*
Blkchokr: *Y?*
TerminX: *Y what?*
Blkchokr: *Y hunt squirrels?*
10 **Dayzd:** *Eat them.*
TerminX: *U never 8 squirrel?*
Blkchokr: *Gross, and neither have U, Trm.*
Dayzd: *How come when my granddad was a kid, kids didn't go 2 school and kill people?*
15 **Rebooto:** *MayB they nu it was wrong.*
TerminX: *U think Klebold and Harris didn't know it was wrong in Littleton?*
Rebooto: *Then Y?*
Dayzd: *Nothing better 2 do.*
20 **TerminX:** *K&H didn't care. Want 2 know what's different between now and 50 years ago? Back then kids cared.*
Blkchokr: *What about?*

Several studies have shown that the appearance on television and in the movies of semiautomatic guns like the Bren 10 and TEC-9
25 boosted sales of those weapons.

Making a Killing

---

1 **gunz:** *guns.*   5 **WY:** Abk. für *Wyoming* (Bundesstaat im Nordwesten der USA).   6 **.22:** Kaliber von 0,22 *inches* (55 mm).   11 **8:** *ate.*
15 **mayB:** *maybe.*   **nu:** *knew.*
[Subtext]   24 **Bren 10:** halbautomatische Pistole vom Kaliber 10 mm des Herstellers Smith and Wesson.   25 **to boost:** fördern.

Dayzd: *Santa Clauz.*

TerminX: *They believed in crap. Don't ask me what, 'cause whatever it was is gone now. Back then U had a reason not 2 kill people.*

5 **Blkchokr:** *U don't now?*

Dayzd: *Lethal injection.*

Rebooto: *Milky Ways.*

TerminX: *No 1 cares anymore. No 1 believes. Nothing 2 care about. Nothing 2 believe in.*

10 **Dayzd:** *I believe in love.*

Rebooto: *I'm dyslexic. I believe in doG.*

TerminX: *We're all gonna die. MayB I'll die before U, but sooner or later U'll croak 2.*

Blkchokr: *Duh.*

15 **Dayzd:** *I won't die.*

Rebooto: *I'll come back as an amoeba.*

Sales of the semiautomatic AKS assault rifle increased dramatically after Patrick Edward Purdy killed five children and wounded thirty more on a school playground in California.

20 *Lethal Passage*

---

6 **lethal injection:** tödliche Injektion, Giftspritze (Form der Vollstreckung der Todesstrafe).   7 **milky way:** vermutl.: (sexueller) Höhepunkt (*to be up in the milky way:* im siebten Himmel sein) oder Anspielung auf beliebtes Computerspiel.   8 **1:** one.   11 **dyslexic:** leseschwach.   **doG:** Umkehrung von *God.*   13 **to croak:** abkratzen, sterben.   **2:** too.   14 **duh:** etwa: sag bloß (sarkastische Antwort auf eine banale Aussage).   16 **amoeba:** Amöbe (einzelliges Lebewesen). [Subtext]   17 **AKS assault rifle:** russisches Sturmgewehr.   18 **Purdy:** Patrick Edward P. erschoss 1989 im Alter von 26 Jahren fünf Schulkinder in Stockton (Kalifornien).   20 **"Lethal Passage":** Buchveröffentlichung von 1994; vgl. S. 174; wörtl.: tödlicher Verlauf.

TerminX: *Once U're dead, U're gone and 4gotten. But it'll be a long time before they 4get about Littleton.*

Dayzd: *Huh?*

Blkchokr: *Trm, U think that's Y they did it? 2 B remem-*
5 *bered?*

TerminX: *It's part of it. Remember Jesse James? Al Ca-*
pone?

Blkchokr: *Attila the Hun. Hitler.*

"'Thirty-five years' experience in newspapers convinces me that
10 teenagers are influenced by the news they see and read. I have no
proof of that. It's my belief. Some children see only the front page
of a newspaper, in a box on the street, on the porch or over the
breakfast table. I did not want to take the risk that another front-
page story about another school shooting might cause some un-
15 balanced fifteen-year-old to add one more disaster to the recent
series.'"

Nigel Wade, *Chicago Sun-Times* newspaper editor, on why he
refused to run the story of the Springfield, Oregon,
shooting on the front page, *New York Times*, 5/23/98

---

1 **4gotten:** *forgotten.* 6 **James:** Jesse J. (1847–82), amerikanischer
Bandit; war zunächst auf der Seite der Konföderierten Soldat im Bür-
gerkrieg, gründete dann zusammen mit seinem Bruder und anderen
eine Bande und wurde schließlich von einem Mitglied dieser Bande
erschossen, der die ausgesetzte Belohnung kassieren wollte.
6 f. **Capone:** Al C. (1899–47), bekannter amerikanischer Gangster-
boss; beherrschte die kriminelle Szene Chicagos von 1925 bis 1931,
konnte allerdings nur wegen Steuerhinterziehung verurteilt werden;
starb nach seiner krankheitsbedingten Freilassung an den Spätfolgen
der Syphilis. 8 **Attila the Hun:** auch als Geißel Gottes bekannter
Hunnenkönig; herrschte von 432 bis zu seinem Tod im Jahr 453.
[Subtext] 12 **porch:** Veranda. 17 **"Chicago Sun-Times":** US-amerikanische Tageszeitung mit einer Auflage von etwa 500 000. 18 **to**
run: (Bericht) bringen, abdrucken.

76

Rebooto: *That creep who 8 people.*
Dayzd: *Dahmer.*
Blkchokr: *Impressed, Dayz.*
Dayzd: *I can C it, Trm. The combo plate. Get the butt-*
5 *holes who make Ur life miserable. Plus Ur name in his-*
tory. And "nothing really matters … to me."
TerminX: *Starts 2 look good. U get them. They get what*
they deserve. Plus U're famous.
Dayzd: *Infamous.*
10 **Rebooto:** *Like President Clinton!*
Blkchokr: *O. J. Simpson.*
Dayzd: *Michael Jackson.*
Rebooto: *That's sick.*
TerminX: *13 kids went down in Littleton. Who do U re-*
15 *member?*
Dayzd: *Klebold and Harris.*
TerminX: *I rest my case.*

At the end of ninth grade we had this awards assembly. It was for everything, not just sports. I was sit-
20 ting with the guys on the [football] team. Principal

---

2 **Dahmer:** Jeffrey D. (1960–94), siebzehnfacher Massenmörder aus
Milwaukee (Wisconsin); 1991 festgenommen und 1994 von einem Mit-
häftling ermordet.   4 **C:** *see.*   **combo plate:** *combination plate:* etwa:
alle auf einen Schlag; Abrechnung.   4 f. **butthole:** Arschloch.   6 **nothing really matters:** Anspielung auf ein Lied der Popgruppe Queen.
9 **infamous:** berüchtigt.   10 **Clinton:** William Jefferson (»Bill«) C.
(geb. 1946), 42. Präsident der USA 1992–2000.   11 **Simpson:** Oren-
thal James S. (geb. 1947), bekannter amerikanischer Football-Spieler;
1995 in einem spektakulären Prozess von der Anklage des Mordes an
seiner Frau freigesprochen.   12 **Jackson:** Michael J. (geb. 1958), amerikanischer Popstar.   17 **to rest one's case:** sein Plädoyer abschlie-
ßen.   18 f. **awards assembly:** Zeremonie zur Preisverleihung am
Schuljahresende.

Curry announced the awards for the speech and debate team, and these kids started to go up on stage. So, you know, these were the brainy kids, and some of them looked okay, but a couple of them were wearing thick glasses and had funny builds. So the guys on the football team start booing. It was just plain stupid. I recall I actually felt embarrassed. I think I even bent my head down so people would see that I wasn't one of them. But it was like a glimpse at how those other kids must have felt, you know? Could you imagine the speech and debate team booing when the football players got their awards? There would be a massacre.

Dustin Williams

---

3 **brainy:** schlau, gescheit, helle.   5 **build:** Körperbau.   6 **to boo:** (aus)buhen.

Tenth Grade

We moved to Middletown at the end of ninth grade,
so tenth grade was my first year here. It's so different
from my old school. You expect it to be different, but
what surprised me was the *way* it was different. It's
just a lot more rigid here. It's like, are you in the
popular crowd or not? There was a popular crowd at
my old school, too, but they were still nice to most
people. They didn't act like if you weren't one of
them you didn't deserve to exist.

I remember coming home after the first week and
telling my mom I didn't like it. Some of the kids just
weren't nice at all. They'd push and curse in the hall,
and it didn't seem like any of the teachers really went

"'There has never ... been a cohort of kids that is so little affected
by adult guidance and so attuned to a peer world. ... We have removed grown-up wisdom and allowed [children] to drift into a
self-constructed, highly relativistic world of friendship and
peers.'"

Prof. William Damon, Stanford University, *New York Times*,
10/3/99

---

6 **rigid:** streng.
[Subtext]   15 **cohort:** Kohorte, Trupp.   16 **to be attuned to s.th.:**
eingestimmt auf etwas sein.   **peer world:** Welt der Gleichaltrigen.
20 **Stanford University:** hoch angesehene, liberale Universität in San
Francisco.

out of their way to stop it. Mom said to lie low. I've always been pretty good at making friends, and she knew I'd find some at Middletown High. She said I only had three years to go. I remember thinking it sounded like
5 an eternity.

Chelsea Baker, a transfer student to Middletown
High School

One thing I don't think a lot of people on the outside realize is how incredibly hard a football team trains.
10 The hours of practice on the weekdays and weekends. Learning forty or fifty plays in your playbook, plus each week studying the films of the team you're facing that Friday night. On top of that you've got schoolwork. And the weight and strength training you
15 have to do on your own just to survive out there. The pressure is huge, and to be honest, there are guys who … well, the only way they have to blow off steam is fighting.

Dustin Williams

20 I always felt Brendan and I had a special connection, even after the point, around the beginning of tenth grade, when we didn't talk much anymore. Maybe it went back to seventh grade, when we were both new. Maybe it was because we were both quote, unquote
25 "outcasts." Anyway, you know how Brendan always

---

1 **to lie low:** sich zurückhalten, unauffällig verhalten.   5 **eternity:** Ewigkeit.   6 **transfer student:** Schulwechsler(in).   11 **playbook:** hier: Handbuch mit Spielzügen und taktischen Hinweisen.   14 **schoolwork:** Hausaufgaben.   17 **to blow off steam:** Dampf ablassen.

seemed to attract trouble. There was just something
about him. Every slight, real or imagined, made his
fur go up. And he couldn't back down. I mean, it
wasn't like he was trying to prove how tough he was. I
5 really think there was something in him. He was helpless to resist it. Even when he was scared silly, he had
to stand up to it.

Emily Kirsch

A lot of what they're saying about the football
10 players is a load of crap. So what if we wore our jer-
seys to school on game days? All we were doing was
trying to get some school spirit going. I've got news
for you. You're out there on the field banging heads
with some 220-pound lineman for four quarters, you
15 need some support from the stands. But it wasn't like
it was a rule. If you didn't want to have school spirit,
that was your business. But some of those guys went
further than that. It was like they wanted to destroy
school spirit.

Sam Flach
20

It's important that you look at this realistically. The
issue of school spirit is certainly a factor in the ten-
sions between these two groups of kids, but you have
to believe it's been blown out of proportion. You're
25 not going to have cheerleaders for the chess team.

2f. **to make s.o.'s fur go up:** jdn. dazu bringen, dass sich ihm, ihr das Fell
sträubt; jdn. wütend machen.   10f. **jersey:** Trikot.   13 **to bang:** zu-
sammenknallen.   14 **lineman:** Spieler am Ende einer Reihe von Spie-
lern im Gedränge (American Football).   **quarter:** Viertel (Spielab-
schnitt).   25 **chess:** Schach.

You're not going to fill the bleachers with fans who cheer when a kid from Middletown takes his opponent's rook. Even the chess players don't want that. Of course we want to produce scholars and we take pride in our National Honor Society members. But that's a matter of school pride, and it's different from school spirit.

Dick Flanagan

When you're with someone a lot, they can change, but it's gradual, so you're not always aware of it. I think that's what happened to all of us, but more to Brendan. Looking back on it, I realize he just got weirder and more and more twisted. It was like he stopped caring. He'd do whatever he wanted.

There was one night when Gary wasn't around. I think maybe he had to go see some psychologist with his mom. Brendan called up and wanted to go out. I'm older than most of the kids in my grade and I have a license, so I usually drive. Anyway, I supplied the car and Brendan supplied the booze. It was probably screwdrivers. We went up to the park and drank for a while

---

Approximately 750,000 deaths by firearms have occurred in this country since 1960.

---

1 **bleachers** (pl.): unüberdachte Zuschauertribüne.   3 **rook:** Turm.
4 **scholar:** Gelehrte(r).   5 **National Honor Society:** 1921 gegründete Gesellschaft zur Förderung und Prämierung besonders begabter und leistungsstarker Schülerinnen und Schüler.   13 **twisted** (fig.): verdreht.   18f. **license:** *driver's license:* Führerschein (in den USA schon von Sechzehnjährigen zu erwerben).   20 **booze:** was zu Saufen; Alkohol.   20f. **screwdriver:** Wodka mit Orangensaft.

and talked. I can't remember now what we talked about, but with Brendan it was usually about how much he hated school and town and blah, blah, blah. Sometimes when I had a good buzz going, I could just
5 tune him out.

After a while Brendan wanted to get in the car again. We drove out of the park, and I thought we'd head back toward town, but he wanted to go the other way. The other way is basically nowhere. Just dark roads and
10 farms and hills, but by then I was pretty trashed and couldn't have cared less.

We're driving alone this road way out in the country, and it's a pretty cool night, so I'm kind of surprised when Brendan rolls down the window.
15 I guess I was sort of aware that he took something out of his jacket. When I heard the bang, I thought one of the tires had blown out or Brendan had thrown a firecracker out of the window. That's what it sounded like. Not really loud or anything. Then we came to the
20 railroad crossing. The red lights were blinking and the gates were coming down, and out of the corner of my eye there's a bright flash and I hear *Bang! Bang!* Only it's louder because we're stopped, and then there's the sound of glass shattering. That's when I realized Bren-
25 dan was shooting at things.

Five percent of students say they've seen another student with a gun in school.

---

4 **to have a good buzz going:** einen im Tee haben, beschwipst sein.
5 **to tune s.o. out:** jdn. ausblenden.   10 **trashed:** kaputt, fertig.
17 **to blow out:** platzen.   18 **firecracker:** Knallkörper.   24 **to shatter:**
(zer)splittern.

Bang! Bang! He shot out the other light. You know the smell of burned gunpowder? Then he looked across the seat at me and smiled. I was beyond caring. The railroad gates went up, and we kept driving. Bren-
5 dan kept shooting. Mostly at signs. Then he opened the glove compartment so he had light while he put more bullets in the clip, or whatever they call it. The gun looked bigger and squarer than the one he'd showed us that time in the park.

10 I never said a word. I didn't tell him to stop. I didn't turn around and go back to town. To be honest, I just didn't care. I actually thought it was a little cool. Like we were a couple of outlaws on the run in *Natural Born Killers*.

15 After a while it was late and we did head back to town. By the time we got to Brendan's, just about every house on his street was dark. Everyone was asleep. Brendan and I sat for a while in the car. You could still smell the gunpowder. I realized that since we'd started
20 driving, he'd hardly said a word.

He looked across the seat at me again. I hope this doesn't sound sick, but it was a really sexy moment. I mean, he really was an outlaw and dangerous and un-predictable, and I happen to find that extremely attrac-

---

25 Twelve percent of students say they know another student who has brought a gun to school.

---

2 **gunpowder:** Schießpulver. 7 **clip:** Magazin. 13 **outlaw:** Geset-zesbrecher, Bandit. **on the run:** auf der Flucht. 13f. **"Natural Born Killers":** Kultfilm von Oliver Stone aus dem Jahr 1994 über Ge-walt und Massenmord. 23f. **unpredictable:** unvorhersehbar.

tive. I think he knew that. He started to move toward me, and I'm thinking, *This is my boyfriend's best friend. I don't believe this.* But I really don't think he cared. I really don't.

5   Anyway, I know this will sound weird after everything I've just said, but I wouldn't let him touch me. I still don't know why. I think maybe it was that dark thing inside him. He could be sexy and attractive, but it was too scary.

10   *Allison Findley*

The school I came from had the same crowds as Middletown. There were athletes and brains and preppies and rah-rah girls and stoners. There were cliques, but they weren't that big of a deal. Sometimes
15 I felt like the real power of a clique was only in the minds of those kids who wished they were in it. If you didn't care, you just went along with your life. At least, at my old school.

                                             Chelsea Baker

20 In ninth grade we might have done some drinking once or twice a month and smoked some pot or hash now and then. By tenth grade we were smashed every Friday and Saturday night. We were getting high in school. A couple of times we dropped acid in eighth
25 period so we'd have a nice buzz going by the time

---

9 **scary:** unheimlich.   13 **rah-rah:** bedingungsloser, unkritischer Fan. **stoner:** Junkie, Drogenabhängige(r).   21 **pot:** Gras, Marihuana. **hash:** Haschisch.   22 **to be smashed:** ordentlich high sein; völlig besoffen sein.   24 **to drop acid:** einen LSD-Trip werfen, LSD nehmen (*acid* [slang]: LSD).   25 **period:** (Schul-)Stunde.

school was over. Oh, and I'm not just talking about
Brendan, Allison, Gary, and me. This was a lot of
kids. Athletes, too.

Ryan Clancy

5 I'm not so far from being a teenager myself, and I can
tell you that there's a huge amount of denial among
parents. Anyone who insists that "my kid isn't drinking, my kid isn't smoking pot, my kid isn't having
sex." Maybe they're right. But look at the statistics
10 and you'll know they can't all be right.

F. Douglas Ellin

TerminX: *Ever C a dead person?*
Blkchokr: *In a casket.*
TerminX: *What was it like?*
15 **Blkchokr:** *It was my grandma. Not a lot different than
when she was alive.*
Dayzd: *LOL.*
Rebooto: *You can go C my grandparents, Trm. They're al-
most dead.*
20 **TerminX:** *I mean it.*
Dayzd: *What?*
TerminX: *A dead person. Spark gone. Lifeless flesh.*
Blkchokr: *I don't want 2 talk about this.*
TerminX: *Y?*

---

25 Of the male youths who say it would be easy to obtain a gun,
most say they can get a gun within twenty-four hours.

---

13 **casket:** Kiste, Sarg.   22 **spark gone:** (Lebens-)Licht aus.

Blkchokr: *So what's tomorrow's weather supposed 2 B?*
TerminX: *Scares U?*
Blkchokr: *Bothers me.*
Dayzd: *I can C it.*
5 **Rebooto:** *What's 2 C?*
Dayzd: *Eternal peace.*
Rebooto: *Eternal nothingness.*
TerminX: *Same difference.*
Blkchokr: *I'm outahere.*
10 **Dayzd:** *Later, Blk.*
Rebooto: *Bye, Blk.*
TerminX: *Imagine death.*
Dayzd: *No pain.*
Rebooto: *No gain.*
15 **TerminX:** *Insane.*

Everything seemed to get more extreme [in tenth
grade]. The battle lines became more clearly drawn,
you know? I think a lot of things contributed to it.
The Middletown Marauders went to the states that
20 fall. It was the furthest a team from Middletown had
gone in twenty-five years, and we were feeling pretty
full of ourselves. We deserved it, considering how
hard we'd worked. But it was kind of like Brendan
and Gary were on a campaign to belittle what we'd
25 done. Make it seem as if what we'd accomplished was
meaningless and that we were basically just a bunch
of dumb jocks with no future. They never said it in

---

1 **2 B:** *to be.*   6 **eternal:** ewig.   7 **nothingness:** Nichts.   9 **outahere:**
out of here.   10 **later:** *see you later.*   17 **battle line:** Schlachtlinie.
19 **to go to the states:** sich für die nationale (Football-)Meisterschaft
qualifizieren.   24 **to belittle:** heruntermachen.

words. It was all done with looks and smirks and sniggers. But the football players heard them loud and clear.

Dustin Williams

5 The weird thing is this year I actually started to make friends with some of the quote, unquote "popular" girls. I'm not really sure why. I think maybe it happened because I don't judge people and they were sick of being in a crowd where they were judged all
10 the time. Like, how cool is your car and how many free minutes do you get on your cell phone? I mean, who cares?

But sometimes they forget. Like the whole judgment thing is so ingrained in them they can't help it. I have a
15 friend who has lots of piercings and he wears black all the time and he likes heavy metal. I was with him one day in the hall, and my "popular" friends gave me these looks. I saw them later and they were like, "How could you talk to him? How could you even acknowledge his
20 presence?" They just couldn't shake it.

Emily Kirsch

Our school puts a significant emphasis on sports. I'm in the English department, and you can imagine how it feels when you hear that they've hired a private
25 plane for $ 25,000 to take the team to a game. Do you have any idea how many classroom sets of Guterson, Shakespeare, and Lowry that would buy? But you

---

2 **snigger:** Gekicher.   11 **cell phone:** Handy.   14 **to be ingrained:** (fig.) verwurzelt sein.   20 **to shake s.th.:** über etwas hinwegkommen.   26 **Guterson:** David G. (geb. 1956), amerikanischer Autor.

also have to understand that a lot of these boys would be lost without athletics. They are simply never going to be scholars. This is the playing field where they've chosen to compete, and unfortunately it's a lot more expensive than an English classroom. These boys are not studious; many of them will not go to college. A great season here may be the highlight of their life. But even if it isn't, the lessons they learn about work and discipline on the team will serve them well in whatever they do. It just may be that for these boys those lessons are more important than Shakespeare's sonnets.

Dick Flanagan

At my old school you didn't have this feeling that one crowd was so totally in power and better than all the rest. It was great if you were a super soccer player, but it was pretty cool if you could make your own movie, or draw or act or play the guitar really well. And it was just dumb to put someone down because they got good grades. But here, it's like the only thing that matters is sports. You get straight A's and people dump on you. It doesn't make sense.

Chelsea Baker

Running a school is like running a business. I know this may sound crass, but you're producing a product.

---

1 **Lowry:** Malcolm L. (1909–57), englischer Autor. 7 **studious:** lernbegierig, fleißig. 8 **highlight:** Höhepunkt. 20 **to put s.o. down:** jdn. fertig machen. 23 **to dump on s.o.:** jdn. von oben herab behandeln. 26 **crass:** krass, unfein, extrem.

In our case, that product is a high school senior who is prepared to go on in the world and be successful in the community. So, in a way, you can say that we have to produce a product that the community approves of,
5 that they will buy into. Sure, I would love to be Edward James Olmos in *Stand and Deliver* and produce a bunch of kids who value calculus over athletics, but if that's not what the community wants, I'll be out of a job.
10   *Allen Curry*

Being on the football team made you special, and some guys definitely took advantage of that. They'd be late for class or curse right in front of a teacher, even in front of an administrator, and nothing serious
15 would happen. Some of these guys acted like they ruled the school. It affected the way a lot of kids looked at us, especially the younger kids. It was like, "Hey, if I make the team, I can get away with that stuff too." Be honest, deep down inside, who doesn't
20 want to be in the spotlight? Who doesn't want to see their picture in the *Middletown Reporter*? It was a real temptation, and if you wanted to take advantage of it, yould could have a great life. Believe me, it was

---

1 **senior:** Zwölftklässler(in).   5 **to buy into s.th.** (infml.): etwas akzeptieren, schlucken.   6 **Olmos:** Edward James O. (geb. 1947), amerikanischer Schauspieler.   **"Stand and Deliver":** etwa: Her mit dem Zeug; Film aus dem Jahr 1988 über den Lehrerfolg eines amerikanischen Mathematiklehrers.   7 **calculus:** Analysis, Differentialrechnung.   18 **to get away with s.th.:** sich etwas leisten, erlauben können.   20 **to be in the spotlight:** im Rampenlicht, Mittelpunkt stehen.

a lot harder not to get a swelled head than to let yourself have one.

Dustin Williams

They talked about guns and they talked about bombs.
5 Gary and I were in McDonald's once and someone
left a newspaper on the table, and there was something about bombing an abortion clinic in it. So
Gary's like, "How do they do it?"

And I'm like, "How do they do what?"
10 And he says, "Make those bombs."

So I go, "Maybe they go to bomb school."

A couple of days later he said he wanted to go to the
public library. And I'm like, "What for?"

And he's like, "I want to look at some books, maybe
15 go on-line."

And I'm like, "You can do that at home."

But he says he has to do it at the library. I think he

In 1990 the Colt firearms company was on the brink of going out
of business. One of the reasons was that federal officials had
20 banned the production of the company's AR-15 semiautomatic
assault rifle. Hundreds of jobs would be lost if the company
closed. The state of Connecticut used state pension funds to purchase 47 percent of the company and save it from going bankrupt. Colt used the money to market a new, slightly modified ver-
25 sion of the assault rifle, now called the Sporter.

---

1 **to get a swelled head:** überheblich werden, die Nase hoch tragen.
7 **abortion:** Abtreibung.   11 **So I go:** Da sag ich.
[Subtext]   18 f. **to go out of business:** bankrott machen.   22 **state
pension funds** (pl.): staatlicher Rentenfond.   23 f. **bankrupt:** bankrott.

said something about not wanting anyone to trace it back to his computer. He could be a little strange.

We're in the library, and I'm over by the magazines, looking at all these stupid pictures of skinny, perfect
5 girls with perfect hair and skin. It makes you wonder why all the rest of us don't just crawl in some hole and do the world a favor and die. Anyway, Gary comes by with this big grin on his face, and I go, "What?"

And he's like, "Not here. Outside."

10 We get outside and he starts laughing, like, "You can't believe this, Allison. I found everything I need to know."

"Need to know about what?" I ask.

And he goes, "About making a bomb. Right in the
15 good old library."

I'm not sure which he thought was cooler: the fact that he found the information, or the fact that he found it in the library.

Allison Findley

20 Everyone's painting this picture of Brendan being the leader and Gary following, but there's another side to it. Especially where those pipe bombs are concerned.

"It is the wisdom and judgment of the [Connecticut State] General Assembly that the Sporter is an assault rifle – it's just the AR-15
25 with a different name."

Rep. Robert Godfrey

---

22 **pipe bomb:** Rohrbombe.
[Subtext] 23 f. **General Assembly:** hier: (Landes-)Parlament. 26 **Rep.:** Abk. für *Representative:* Mitglied des Repräsentantenhauses eines Bundesstaates.

Brendan wasn't mechanical. I mean, he just wasn't interested in that kind of thing. But Gary loved building stuff. He really had a talent for it. I remember going to his house for a birthday party and seeing what he'd
5 done with LEGOs. He'd made LEGO robots and programmed them with his computer, so if they walked into something, they could turn around and go in another direction. It was pretty awesome. You hear the police reports about how well constructed
10 and intricate those pipe bombs were. I guarantee you, that was Gary's work.

Ryan Clancy

I had to take him to the hardware store and over the state line, where they sell fireworks. When we got to
15 the [fireworks] stand, that was probably about the most excited I'd ever seen him. He wanted to know which ones had the most gunpowder. They told him, and those were the ones he bought.

Allison Findley

---

20 "We say we want to regulate assault guns; then we go out and buy an assault gun factory. ... The whole darn thing is so hypocritical it's hard to imagine."

Rep. David Oliver Thorp

---

8 **awesome:** irre; beeindruckend. 10 **intricate:** kompliziert. 13 **hardware store:** Haushaltswarengeschäft. 13 f. **over the state line:** auf der anderen Seite der (Bundesstaaten-)Grenze.
[Subtext] 20 **to regulate:** (staatlich) regeln. 21 **darn:** verflixt, verdammt. 21 f. **hypocritical:** heuchlerisch.

Brendan and Gary had this big announcement they wanted to make. They were going to announce it on Saturday. So Allison drives up and Gary's in the front seat and Brendan's in the back, and we just take off.
5 Listening to music, smoking, cruising. We probably drive for more than an hour and a half, until we're way out in the middle of nowhere. Then we go down some dirt road, and we're at this cabin. I thought Gary said it was his uncle's, but anyway, no one's
10 around.

So Gary opens the trunk and takes out this green duffel bag and all these big sheets of colored paper, like the kind you do school projects on. And we all go tromping off into the woods. The thing is I have
15 no idea what's going on. I'm like, "So what are we doing today? An art project?" And they're not telling me. It's an announcement, you know? I'm supposed to wait.

We get to some place that Gary likes, and he stops
20 and says, "Okay, we'll do it here." Next thing I know, he's taking pushpins out of the duffel bag, and we're supposed to pin all these sheets of paper up to these trees. Like we're making a multicolored room in the trees that's all paper walls. This probably takes an hour
25 itself. And then Gary has to very carefully number all the sheets and make notes in a notebook. I have no idea what this is about, but so what? It's as good as doing anything else, I guess.

Then Gary says we're ready, and he goes back to the

---

5 **to cruise:** herumfahren.   8 **dirt road:** nicht asphaltierte Straße.
12 **duffel bag:** Sportbeutel, -tasche.   14 **to tromp off:** wegstapfen.
21 **pushpin:** Heftzwecke.

bag and he takes out this thing and sets it on the ground
right in the middle of the paper room we've created.
Then he tells us to get the hell out of there. I ask him
how far, and he says a hundred yards at least. If you
5 want to know the truth, I thought he was nuts. A hundred yards is the length of a football field. It's pretty
obvious by now that he's got some kind of homemade
bomb. But it's kind of fun and goofy to run off into the
woods, so I do it.

10 We go running, and before long we're all bent over
with our hands on our knees, gasping for breath. It's
the smoking. And a little while later Gary comes crashing through the trees, and we yell to him that we're
over here.

15 The thing goes off before he can get to us. There's
this really sharp, loud *thunk*! sound, and I swear a hundred yards away I can actually feel the ground shake
and the leaves in the trees rustle. Now Gary and Brendan take off back toward the "blast zone."

20 So I get there, and I can't believe what I'm seeing.
First of all, every single piece of paper is blown away.
Totally shredded. It's like a big circle of multicolored
paper shreds on the ground around the blast site.
Leaves are blown off the trees, so the leaves and paper
25 are mixed together. The whole place reeks of burned
gunpowder. Twigs are snapped and some of the smaller
branches are broken. You can see that this thing was a

---

5 **to be nuts:** verrückt sein.   7 **homemade:** selbst gebastelt.   11 **to
gasp for breath:** nach Luft ringen, keuchen.   16 **thunk:** plötzlicher,
dumpfer Knall   18 **to rustle:** rascheln.   19 **blast zone:** Explosions-
zone.   22 **shredded:** zerfetzt.   25 **to reek of s.th.:** nach etwas rie-
chen.   26 **twig:** Zweig.   **to snap:** zerbrechen.

lot bigger than it sounded from so far away. Maybe the sound was muffled by the trees and whatnot.

Now Gary says we have to pick up every shred of paper, and he's got rolls of Scotch tape so we can paste them back together. And that's when I figure out what's going on: We're re-creating the scene. Like what they did with that 747 that blew up and they couldn't figure out why.

So now we have to gather up all these little colored shreds of paper and try to tape them together. The thing is maybe you can do it with some of the larger pieces, but the smaller pieces are impossible, and it's not like we haven't been drinking screwdrivers from a plastic half-gallon milk container we brought along.

Finally Brendan says the hell with it. Gary's the only one who doesn't want to stop. If it were up to him, he'd stay out there for a week until every single shred was taped back together. He wants to see the blast pattern, he wants to make sure they built the bomb right. Brendan says, "Look, if we didn't build it right, you think there'd be all this shredded paper and leaves and branches everywhere?"

And Gary's like, "Yeah, but I still want to see." Brendan and I quit and just sit and drink and smoke and watch Allison and Gary pick and tape and pick and tape until even Allison's tired of it. You can see it's

---

2 **to muffle:** (Geräusch) dämpfen. **and whatnot:** und so, und was auch immer. 4 **Scotch tape:** Markenname für ein Klebeband; Tesafilm. 7 **747:** Boeing 747; Jumbo. 14 **half-gallon:** Hohlmaß; etwa: 1,9 l (in den USA). 19 **blast pattern:** Explosionsmuster, Trefferbild.

hopeless, but Gary is like a fanatic. He just has to see the blast pattern.

Brendan, Allison, and I go back to the cabin, and the door's locked, so Brendan gets the tire iron out of Allison's car and uses it to pry the door open. He pretty much destroys the lock, but we're too trashed to care. We go in and hang around and eat some of the food in the fridge and watch TV. After a while Gary shows up and he's like, okay, he's seen enough. He declares it a success.

He says we should go, and I say, "Well, shouldn't we at least fix the door so your uncle won't have a total fit?" And Gary's like, "Uncle? I don't have any uncle." Can you believe it?

Anyway, we get in the car and start driving back, and all the way they're talking about who they're gonna blow up with these bombs. And it's a pretty good-size list. The only thing is they really meant it.

Ryan Clancy

TerminX: *Pretty awesome 2day, huh? A couple of those suckas in school would put a lot of jerks out of their misery.*

Blkchokr: *Plus a few non-jerks.*

Dayzd: *Civilian casualties.*

TerminX: *Collateral damage.*

---

4 **tire iron:** Wagenheber. 5 **to pry open:** aufbrechen. 12f. **total fit:** totaler (Wut-)Anfall. 17 **good-size:** groß, stattlich. 21f. **to put s.o. out of his, her misery:** jdn. aus seinem, ihrem Elend erlösen. 24 **civilian casualty:** Verlust unter der Zivilbevölkerung. 25 **collateral damage:** Kollateralschaden, (unbeabsichtigter) Folgeschaden.

Rebooto: *U guys need 2 make a smart bomb.*

Dayzd: *Smart bomb 4 dumb jocks.*

TerminX: *B cool if U could convert that semiautomatic into fully automatic.*

5 **Dayzd:** *Need a hellfire switch.*

Rebooto: *What R U talking about?*

Dayzd: *You get a 50-round clip, it's almost the same thing.*

TerminX: *Jungle-clip them. Then it's 100 rounds.*

10 **Rebooto:** *Hello?*

Blkchokr: *Gunz, Booto.*

Rebooto: *:-o*

TerminX: *I read the marines use a special version of "Doom" 2 train soldiers.*

15 **Dayzd:** *1-shot kills?*

TerminX: *Head and upper-torso shots.*

Blkchokr: *Seen any good movies lately?*

Rebooto: *Read any good books?*

Dayzd: *"Unforgiven."*

20 **Rebooto:** *O yeah!*

Blkchokr: *Weird flick.*

Dayzd: *Y?*

Blkchokr: *Couldn't C the message.*

TerminX: *When a real man has a problem, he gets a gun.*

---

5 **hellfire switch:** Schalter zur Aufrüstung einer halbautomatischen zu einer automatischen Waffe.   6 **R U:** *are you.*   9 **to jungle-clip:** mit einem Doppelmagazin ausrüsten.   **round:** Schuss.   12 **:-o:** Zeichen für: staun (Gefühlsausdruck).   13 **marines** (pl.): Marineinfanterie.   15 **1-shot:** mit einem Schuss.   16 **upper-torso:** Oberkörper.   19 **"Unforgiven":** Buch zu dem Film *The Unforgiven* (dt. *Gnadenlos*) aus dem Jahr 1992 mit Clint Eastwood, Gene Hackman und Morgan Freeman über einen alternden Berufskiller, der noch einen letzten Auftrag annimmt.   21 **flick:** Film, Streifen.

Rebooto: *U C where they want 2 expand the movie ratings so they have warnings like cigarettes?*
TerminX: *Stupid. It doesn't work with cigarettes.*
Blkchokr: *They're on booze, 2.*
5 **Dayzd:** *Warning: Uncontrolled firearm use may be hazardous to your health.*
Blkchokr: *LOL!*

There are probably about 150 million law-abiding
American citizens who enjoy watching football. My-
10 self included. The idea that this incident can somehow
be blamed on football is sadly mistaken. These were
two sick, disturbed boys. Like many people I know, I
also happen to own several hunting rifles and a handgun I keep in my home for personal protection. Is it
15 locked? No, but it's hidden. If I ever have to defend
my home against someone trying to break in, the time
it takes me to unlock a gun might just be the difference between the life and death of my children.

The Second Amendment to the Constitution gives
20 us the right to bear arms. Are you going to change the
Constitution? Why stop at the Second Amendment?
Why not throw out the First Amendment, too? Who

A gun kept in the home is forty-three times more likely to kill
someone you know than to kill a stranger in self-defense.

25   *Lethal Passage*

---

1 f. **movie rating:** (staatliche) Filmbewertung.   5 f. **hazardous:** gefähr-
lich.   8 **law-abiding:** gesetzestreu.   19 **Second Amendment:** Zweiter
Verfassungszusatz (beinhaltet das Recht jedes erwachsenen Amerika-
ners auf Waffenbesitz).   22 **to throw out:** abschaffen.

needs freedom of speech? Hey, who needs the right to
vote? See where this is going?

Dick Flanagan

It's horrible when kids are killed in schools. It's a
nightmare. Obviously, after what happened, I should
know. But if you want to save kids' lives, you'll save
a lot more by raising the driving age than banning
guns.

Allen Curry

Death by Car Vs. Death by Gun
More people die in car accidents than from guns. But the
numbers are closer than you might think. In 1995 in many states
there were almost as many deaths by firearms as there were traffic
fatalities. In the following states there were actually more deaths
by firearms.

State	Traffic-Related Deaths	Firearm Deaths
Arizona	977	986
California	4,314	4,805
District of Columbia	67	269
Louisiana	899	1,087
Maryland	673	760
Nevada	298	398
Virginia	902	956

(*Source:* Data from the National Vital Statistics system, National
Center for Health Statistics)

[Subtext]   10 **vs.:** Abk. für *versus:* gegen.   14 **fatality:** Todesfall.
16 **traffic-related:** Verkehrs-.   24 **vital statistics** (pl.): Bevölkerungs-
statistik.

It still seems strange to me that I was nobody until Dustin asked me out. I'd be in the girls' room with Deirdre Bunson and some of those other girls, and it was like I didn't even exist. I wasn't on their radar. At
5 my old school you'd say hi to someone even if you didn't know them. Here you say hi and it's like, "Do I know you?"

Chelsea Baker

I'm sure you've heard about that fight at Dustin's
10 house. If you want to know the truth, up to that point, that was one of the scariest things I'd ever seen. The thing is I always knew [Sam] Flach was mean and strong, but this was just beyond anything you could have imagined.
15

Ryan Clancy

I still don't understand why Brendan wanted to go to that party. I mean, he must have felt that Dustin was his neighbor and sort of his friend, but Dustin was on the football team, and everyone knew it was
20 a football party. Some people say Brendan was just asking for it. I don't know. I think it was more like

---

After Michael Carneal killed three and wounded five in a Padu-cah, Kentucky, high school, several magazines and newspapers reported that he had imitated a computer-game pattern by quickly
25 shifting from one target to the next.

---

20 f. **to be just asking for it** (infml.): geradezu danach schreien, es nicht besser verdienen.

Rosa Parks. He was tired of sitting in the back of the bus.

Emily Kirsch

We came around the side of the house. You had to go
5 through this gate because Dustin has a pool in his
backyard. Brendan and I were going in. Sam and
Deirdre were coming out. The thing is it was just, like,
bad timing. Sam got to the gate first. He pushed it
open und just kept going. Like he wasn't even going
10 to bother holding it for Deirdre. So Brendan caught
the gate and held it for her. Some people say he
bowed or touched her on the shoulder or something. I
didn't see it. All I saw was Sam come out of nowhere
and get Brendan from behind.
15

Ryan Clancy

I was in the kitchen and I heard the shouting. I came
out, and Sam had Brendan on the ground and was
smashing him like a wild animal. There had to be six
guys standing around watching. Any one of them
20 could have pulled Sam off, but they didn't. I had to
get Sam in a choke hold and practically suffocate him
to get him to stop.

Dustin Williams

---

1 **Rosa Parks:** Mit ihrer Weigerung, einem weißen Fahrgast ihren Sitz-
platz im Bus abzutreten, leitete die Afro-Amerikanerin Rosa Parks im
Jahr 1955 in Montgomery (Alabama) erste Reformen der Rassenge-
setzgebung in den Vereinigten Staaten ein.   1 f. **to sit in the back of
the bus:** (wie Rosa Parks) hinten im Bus sitzen; unterprivilegiert
sein.   21 **choke hold:** Schwitzkasten.   **to suffocate:** (er)würgen, er-
sticken.

Have you ever heard the sound of a fist on bone? It would make you sick. One thing I know for certain, Sam was definitely going for Brendan's face. I swear if I'd had a gun that night, I would have shot Sam myself.

Ryan Clancy

I went home that night and told my mom there was something really wrong with these kids.

Chelsea Baker

It wasn't like that in elementary school. I mean, even when two kids got into a fight, they didn't try to hurt each other so badly. Kids in elementary school are way more open to teachers' influence than when they get to middle school and high school. Why can't they teach something in elementary school that could help kids learn how to deal with one another without it always becoming violent?

Emily Kirsch

I heard about it in the teachers' room first thing Monday morning. A little later I saw Brendan in the hall. His nose was swollen, and his lip was fat and split,

---

It was reported that Carneal wounded or killed eight people with eight bullets, despite the fact that he'd never fired a gun before. This was not the case. It was later discovered that Carneal had learned to shoot at a summer camp run by a well-known national youth organization.

---

21 **fat:** hier: dick angeschwollen.

and his eye was black and blue. A few minutes later I
saw Sam. Not a scratch. You never would've known
he'd been in a fight.

Beth Bender

5 Boys fight. They've always fought and they always
will fight. Was Sam provoked? Who knows. We
weren't there. We didn't see. Forgive me if I sound
callous, but this was an incident that took place off
school property.

10
Allen Curry

Gary was really down. I didn't know why. It could
have been something at home, I'll never know. We
were talking on the phone about what happened to
Brendan at the party and how the jocks just stood
15 around and didn't stop Sam. Gary said he wished
they'd all die. I said, "Not really, right?" He said he
really, really did want them to die slow, painful, miserable deaths. I said, "While you live to be a hundred?"
He said he really didn't care. He was past the point of
20 caring. He just wanted them to die.

Allison Findley

Michael Carneal was frequently picked on and teased. The intimation that he was gay was even printed in his school's newspaper.

---

25 According to several news organizations, Michael Carneal carried
a backpack containing more than five hundred rounds of ammunition on the day he killed.

---

8 **callous:** gefühllos, hartherzig.
[Subtext] 22f. **intimation:** Andeutung.   23 **gay** (infml.): homosexuell.

The Day It Happened

Brendan called me around dinnertime. It was definitely weird. I don't think we'd spoken on the phone since the end of ninth grade. There was a time when I
5 was pretty sure he was interested in me in a romantic way. But I thought that had passed. Anyway, we talked for a while, and I wasn't sure what he was getting at. Then he told me that about a week before the fight with Sam he'd been rejected by a private mili-
10 tary school he'd applied to.

I know that must sound totally out of character. I wonder if Gary even knew. I mean, why in the world would a kid like Brendan want to go to military school? But I think somewhere inside he knew he was headed
15 for big trouble, and he must have believed that military school might be the way to save himself. And if I'm right, then when he was rejected, it was like he lost his last lifeline. Being rejected meant two more years of living hell at Middletown High. I think he knew he'd
20 never survive it. I think maybe that was the last straw. He lost hope.

We talked for about twenty minutes, and then he asked me if I was going to the dance that night, and I

---

10 **to apply to s.th.:** sich bei etwas bewerben.   11 **out of character:** untypisch.   14f. **to be headed for s.th.:** todsicher in etwas geraten.
18 **lifeline:** hier: Rettungsanker.

was like, "No way." He asked if I was sure, because he'd noticed that I was getting friendly with some of the quote, unquote "popular" girls. I assured him there was absolutely, positively no way I was going.

5 And then he said he was glad, and that he'd always liked me. And then he said good-bye.

Emily Kirsch

I can see how Gary might have been thinking about killing himself. Brendan never struck me that way. It
10 was like he was too angry to do that. He wanted to get too many people. But if you put them together, you can almost see the idea coming to them. Deciding to do themselves in, but going to school and taking as many of those guys with them as they could.

15 *Ryan Clancy*

To me it was just like any other Friday night. The popular kids were at the dance. Gary and Brendan were gone. I didn't know where. I went over to Block-

---

"Five days before the shooting, Eric [Harris]'s hopes of becoming
20 a marine were undone after his parents told a recruiter about [the antidepressant medicine Eric was taking]. ... Friends said that Eric was crushed by the news, and had been growing increasingly depressed as graduation neared."

New York Times, 6/29/99

---

1 **no way** (adv., infml.): auf gar keinen Fall.   13 **to do o.s. in:** sich umbringen.   18f. **Blockbuster:** Name einer amerikanischen Videothek-Kette; wörtl.: Kassenschlager.
[Subtext]   19f. **to undo s.o.'s hopes:** jds. Hoffnung(en) zunichte machen.   **recruiter:** Rekrutierungssachbearbeiter(in).

buster. I wasn't really looking for a video. I was looking for someone to hook up with for a couple of hours.

Allison Findley

5 It was an unfortunate combination of poor building design and a couple bright minds ingenious enough to take advantage of it. You've got a windowless gym with four main entrances, each consisting of double metal doors. You've got two heavily armed young
10 men who've rigged booby-trap bombs in a way that kept us from getting to the doors from the outside. Inside they chained the doors shut. You want to talk about planning? They brought drinks and snacks for themselves. And flashlights.

Allen Curry
15

You hear people say the boys were crazy. That it was just an insane, unpredictable thing that doesn't happen to the vast majority of people. Like getting hit by lightning. Utterly random. But I don't think so.
20 Every year you hear about kids walking into their

In 1996, 2,866 children and teenagers were murdered with guns, 1,309 committed suicide with guns, and 468 died in unintentional shootings. A total of 4,643 young people were killed by firearms.

---

2 **to hook up with s.o.:** sich jdm. (für kurze Zeit) anschließen.   6 **ingenious:** intelligent, erfindungsreich.   10 **to rig:** anbringen.   **booby-trap bomb:** versteckte Bombe, Sprengladung. 14 **flashlight:** Taschenlampe.
[Subtext]   22 f. **unintentional:** unabsichtlich.

school and shooting classmates and teachers. You
don't hear about them walking into McDonald's and
shooting people. They don't go to the town swimming
pool or the movies and do it. Most of these kids live
in neighborhoods with elementary schools, middle
schools, and high schools. But they don't go to some
other school. They always go to their own school. It's
not random. It's a message, and the sooner we wake
up and listen, the better.

Beth Bender

My father fought in World War Two against the Japa-
nese and the Germans. I realize that it was a long time
ago, but when you face a people in mortal combat, it's
a difficult thing to forget. Sometimes at a gun show I
see those foreign-made weapons. Some of them come
from countries we once considered our enemies. Part
of me can't help thinking that they must be laughing
their heads off at us. They don't have to go to war
against us anymore. All they have to do is sell us

Several newspapers reported that Luke Woodham said he killed
because he felt he was mistreated every day. He said he did it to
show society: "Push us and we will push back."

---

13 **mortal combat:** Kampf auf Leben und Tod.   15 **foreign-made:** im
Ausland hergestellt, ausländisch.   17f. **to laugh one's head off:** sich
totlachen.
[Subtext]   20 **Woodham:** Am 1. 10. 1997 erschoss der 16-jährige
Luke W. seine Mutter und anschließend in der Pearl High School,
Pearl (Mississippi), zwei Schüler und verletzte sieben weitere. Vgl.
S. 170.   21 **to mistreat s.o.:** jdn. schlecht behandeln.

108

guns, and we'll do the job for them. And the darnedest part of it is they make a profit.

Jack Phillips

Blockbuster is right around the corner from school.
So I'm in there looking at titles, hoping someone I
know will walk in. And who comes in? Emily Kirsch.
Like, at first I wasn't even going to talk to her. I went
back to looking at titles. But then I look up and there
she is, right across the aisle. So we say hi, what's up?
You know, the regular BS.

It runs out pretty fast, and there's that moment when
one of you has to come up with something else to say or
you're just going to go off in different directions. And
I swear I still don't know why I said it, but just jok-
ing around, I said, "So, how come you're not at the
dance?"

Like she or I would ever go to a school dance.

And that's when she told me about Brendan calling
her, and how he wanted to make sure she wouldn't be
at the dance. And it just gave me the creepiest feeling.
Why would he say that? Since it wasn't like I had any-

Only a tiny fraction of the guns manufactured in Japan stay in that
country. Japan has very strict gun control laws. The majority of the
guns manufactured in Japan are shipped to the United States.

Making a Killing

---

1 f. **darnedest:** Superlativ von *darned* ›verdammt‹.   9 **aisle:** Gang
(zwischen Reihen).   **what's up?:** was gibt's?   20 **creepy:** unheimlich,
gruselig.

thing better to do, I figured I'd walk over to school and
take a look.

Allison Findley

I heard someone scream and then I saw one of them.
5 He was wearing green camouflage clothing and a
black ski hat pulled down over his face with the eyes
and mouth cut out. At first I thought it was a joke.
Guys dressed like commandos and carrying toy guns.
But then one of them, I think it was probably Bren-
10 dan, fired a bunch of shots at the ceiling. It sounded
like a pack of firecrackers, but you could hear the bullets pinging and ricocheting off the rafters and air-
conditioning ducts. A couple of those big mercury-
vapor lights shattered, and glass started to rain down
15 on us. When that happened, most of the crowd dived
for the floor.

Dustin Williams

Do you know what a semiautomatic is? It looks like a
machine gun. *Only it's smaller and easier to hide.* It
20 sprays out lots of bullets very quickly. I'm told it has
absolutely no use as a hunting weapon and hardly any
accuracy, either. So it serves no purpose in target
shooting. Then what is it for? Why is it made? What
do the companies that make these guns think people
25 are going to do with them?

Beth Bender

---

5 **camouflage:** Tarnung.   8 **commando:** Stoßtruppsoldat.   12 **to
ping:** peng machen.   **to ricochet:** abprallen.   **rafter:** Dachbalken,
Sparren, Träger.   13 **duct:** Schacht.   13f. **mercury-vapour light:**
Quecksilberdampflampe.   15f. **to dive for the floor:** sich auf den Bo-
den werfen.   20 **to spray:** abfeuern.   22 **accuracy:** Zielgenauigkeit.

They were running around and yelling and firing at the ceiling. Bullets were ricocheting all over the place. Glass was shattering. It was, like, total mayhem. They told us to lie facedown on the floor with our hands
5 over our head. That made it hard to see. With all the shouting and firing and running, and with the gym semidark because it was a dance, it was hard to tell how many there really were.

I think I knew almost instantly that one of them was
10 Brendan. And that led to the fairly logical conclusion that Gary would be involved too. I took a couple of guesses at who the others might be. I think a lot of us were surprised when we finally realized there weren't any others. It was just Brendan and Gary. Even with
15 the masks you could tell who was who because Brendan was thin and Gary was sort of chubby. You wouldn't have thought only two of them could make so much noise and gunfire. At first I couldn't understand why they were running and yelling and wearing masks.
20 Now I think it was just to add to the fear factor. Believe me, it worked.

Dustin Williams

They were yelling at us to get away from the doors. That the doors were booby-trapped. They herded us
25 all into the center of the gym and told us to lie face-down. Mr. Curry tried to get stern and tough, and started to tell Gary to put down the gun. Gary didn't

---

3 **mayhem:** Chaos.   7 **semidark:** halbdunkel.   16 **chubby:** pummelig.   24 **to be booby-trapped:** mit versteckten Sprengladungen versehen sein.   **to herd s.o.:** jdn. (zusammen)treiben.   26 **stern:** streng.

say a word. He just fired off half a dozen quick shots at the ceiling. Those bullets ricocheted around up there. One of them came back down so close to my face I could feel the air move. It sounded like that beach scene in *Saving Private Ryan*.

Paul Burns

In this school when they get mad, they pull out that walkie-talkie and point it at you. Like it's a stick or a whip or something. Or maybe it's to make sure you know they can get anyone pronto, even the police. It's like an automatic reflex. Mr. Curry pointed his walkie-talkie at Gary and Brendan. And Brendan just shot him.

Chelsea Baker

"The killers [in school shootings] were able to easily acquire high-powered guns, and in many cases, their parents helped the children get them, either directly or through negligence. **Guns with rapid-fire capability ... that can spray a burst of bullets in a matter of seconds, were used in the incidents with the most victims.**"

New York Times, 6/14/98

---

5 **"Saving Private Ryan":** Film aus dem Jahr 1998 mit Tom Hanks in der Hauptrolle über den Versuch, das Leben eines einfachen Soldaten nach der Landung der Alliierten in der Normandie im Jahr 1944 zu retten (dt. *Der Soldat James Ryan*).   10 **pronto** (adv., infml.): sofort, schnell.
[Subtext]   15 f. **high-powered:** leistungsstark.   17 **negligence:** Fahrlässigkeit.   18 **rapid-fire capability:** Schnellfeuertauglichkeit.   **burst:** Salve.

The bullet went into the right side of my chest. I thought I was going to die. I thought about my wife, Sara, and my kids. But I was incredibly lucky. It's a story you've heard before. Half an inch this way or that and I wouldn't be here talking to you right now. But the good Lord said it wasn't my time.

Allen Curry

Of course I was shocked when I heard the news. Everyone around here was. All I could think about was Samantha and Tom Lawlor, and what sweet, kind people they'd been, and about that day four years ago when Samantha had cried in my kitchen. I don't know what happened to Brendan after they left Springfield, but I knew Samantha and Tom well enough to know that nothing they did could have led to anything that extreme. If you've raised children yourself, then you know you can't blame the parents. If a child doesn't want you to know or see something, then you're not going to know or see it.

Kit Conner

I didn't even know they'd shot Mr. Curry. Most of the kids in the gym didn't know it either. Guns were going off, and people were getting down as fast as they could. Too many things were happening at once.

Dustin Williams

In 1999 not a single person was killed flying on an American airline. More than a dozen were killed by guns in schools.

---

6 **Lord:** Gott.

The police just couldn't believe that it was an accident that I was at the dance. If they'd spend half as much time trying to help kids with their problems as they did trying to prove that I was an accomplice, we prob-
5 ably wouldn't have these kinds of problems in the first place.

Allison Findley

I think there might have been an opportunity, right at the beginning, to confront them, challenge them, get
10 them to lay down their weapons. But they had the el-ement of surprise on their side, and they came in fir-ing and making a lot of noise. Once they shot Allen and had the rest of us on our stomachs, they were in control.
15

Dick Flanagan

I was one of the first ones they put the plastic ties on. "Aw, look, it's Flach on the floor." [Brendan] pressed the barrel of the gun right against the back of my

---

Several years ago the Winchester-Olin company started selling a
20 new bullet called the Black Talon. It was called the Talon because its tip is divided into six "claws" that unfold as it penetrates flesh. While travelling through the body, this increases the diameter of the bullet nearly three times, causing far more damage than an or-dinary bullet.

---

4 **accomplice:** Komplizin, Komplize.   5f. **in the first place:** über-haupt, von vornherein, erst.
[Subtext]   20 **talon:** Kralle.   21 **claw:** Klaue.   22 **diameter:** Durchmesser.

114

head. I thought I was dead meat. Then he yanked my
hands behind my back and pulled that plastic tie
tight. Like a calf-roping contest. Then he kicked me
as hard as he could in the ribs, cracked two of them,
5 as it turned out.

Sam Flach

One of them came over and started putting a tie on
my wrists. I asked which one he was, and he said
Brendan. I said, "Brendan, come on, it's me, Dustin."
10 He said, "Sorry, dude, it's too late."

Dustin Williams

They had it planned perfectly. The way they came in
firing and yelling. The way they tied up some of the
football players and male teachers first. The way they
15 took the walkie-talkies away, and kicked and hurt
some of them. By the time I realized how absurd the
whole thing was, at least five minutes had passed. I sat
up and looked around. There were nearly sixty of us
and two of them. They were still tying up some of the

---

20 "In Jonesboro and Springfield, the parents of the accused assail-
ants followed the general advice of the National Rifle Association
and taught their children, at an early age, how to use guns properly."

New York Times, 6/14/98

---

1 **to yank:** ruckartig zerren. 3 **calf-roping contest:** Wettbewerb beim
Rodeo, bei dem ein Kalb mit dem Lasso eingefangen wird. 10 **dude:**
etwa: Alter, Kumpel.
[Subtext] 20f. **assailant:** Angreifer(in). 21 **National Rifle Association:** Nationale Vereinigung der Gewehrbesitzer(innen).

bigger boys. I didn't know they'd already shot Allen. I
started to get up, and one of them saw me and came
running over, yelling at me to get down. I was scared,
but I didn't back down. He fired at the ceiling and
5 yelled again for me to lie down. He was still wearing
that black mask, but I knew it was Gary. I said, "I'm
not lying down, Gary, and I don't think you'll shoot
me."
He aimed that gun right at my face and said, "I'd hate
10 to shoot you, Ms. Bender, but I will." I said, "I don't
think so." And just like that, he fired. The force of the
blast knocked me down, and I was in terrible pain on
the left side of my head. I didn't know what had happened. I was pretty sure I hadn't been shot. It turned
15 out the bullet missed. But kids all over the gym
started screaming and crying. I lay down again. I hon-
estly believe he intentionally missed the first time, but
I also think he wouldn't have missed a second time.

Beth Bender

---

20 Several newspapers reported that T. J. Solomon had posters of
sports heroes in his room. He was active at his church and at-
tended youth services. One paper reported that he'd led a prayer
the day before he shot and wounded six students.

[Subtext] 20 **Solomon:** Der 15-jährige T. J. Solomon verletzte am
20. 5. 1999 sechs Schüler der Heritage High School in Conyers (Georgia) mit Schusswaffen, die er an Sicherheitsbeamten vorbeigeschmug-
gelt hatte. Vgl. S. 172.

Gary's Suicide Note

Dear Mom,

By the time you read this, I'll be gone. I just want you to know that there's nothing you could have done to stop this. I know you always tried your best for me, and if anyone doubts you, just show them this letter.

I don't know if I can really explain why I did this. I guess it's because I know that I'll never be happy. I know that every day of my life will hurt and be a lot more bad than good. It's entirely a matter of, What's the point of living?

I could have just gone and offed myself quietly, but that would have been an even bigger waste. If I go this way, taking the people who made my life miserable with me, then maybe it will send a message. Maybe something will change, and some other miserable kid like me somewhere will get treated better and maybe find a reason to live.

Mom, I could never tell you how unhappy I was. I knew there was nothing you could do to help, and life has been hard enough on you already. I'm truly, truly sorry that I'm going to put you through so much pain, but I hope that in a year or two you'll get over it. Maybe you could move away and change your name and even have a new kid.

You can start over. I wish I could be there with you, but I'm past the point of no return.

Love forever,
Gary

The Dance

I hid behind the refreshment table. There were three
of us there. The other two were preppy, semipopular
kids. The kind who hang around on the fringes of the
popular clique and get invited in when they need a
crowd, like to a game or a dance or a big party. Those
two were scared !&*#less. I really think they believed
that if Brendan and Gary found them, they'd shoot
them.
                                        Allison Findley

I told them to stop shooting at the ceiling. That a ricocheting bullet could kill someone as easily as an
aimed one. One of them instantly fired off another
burst. He had to know that the ricochets could have
hit him as easily as anyone else. I had to assume he

"Bill [Kinkel, Kip's father] ... hoped buying Kip a legally registered rifle, taking him to a shooting range and seeing that he was
taught to use it properly might actually mitigate against the boy's
unrelenting fascination with firearms."
                                        Rolling Stone, 9/17/98

---

4 **fringe:** Rand.   7 **to be scared !&*#less:** *to be scared shitless:* sich
vor Angst in die Hosen scheißen.   14 **ricochet:** Querschläger.
[Subtext]   17 **shooting range:** Schießplatz.   18 **to mitigate:** mildern,
mäßigen.

didn't care. I think I'm a reasonably good judge of
kids' moods. I can tell when they're putting on an act
and bluffing. Believe me, these boys were not putting
on an act.
₅   *Dick Flanagan*

You want to hear something ironic? The school is
about twenty years old, and I recall that there was
some argument over the size of the gym when the
building designs were first considered. Some people
₁₀ felt it was too large and they were spending too much
money on it. But you want to know why I think no
one was seriously hurt by a ricocheting bullet? Because that gym is so darn big.
                                                  Allen Curry

₁₅ I remember wondering why they didn't start shooting
kids right away. And I thought, *Oh, no, killing us isn't
the point. They have some stupid message they want us
to hear first.*
                                                  Deirdre Bunson

₂₀ Why did they bring flashlights and snacks? Because
they weren't planning just to kill those kids. They
were going to make them suffer. Just like those kids
had made us suffer.
                                                  Allison Findley

₂₅ I've got pretty broad shoulders, but my arms are short
because I'm stocky and not all that tall. Plus they're

26 **stocky:** stämmig.

pretty bulked up from lifting [weights]. It's actually
not that easy for me to cross my hands behind my
back. They put a tie around my wrists, but it wasn't all
that tight. I had some wiggle room.

5

Paul Burns

Was I surprised when I heard about it? Yeah, for like
a second, but not really. Look at it as a form of torture. Day in and day out. Society makes you go to
school, and then the society in school tortures you.
10 You realize there's no way out. Everyone has a
breaking point. Sooner or later everyone will snap.
Maybe if Brendan and Gary hadn't snapped, someone else would have.

Ryan Clancy

15 The first bomb went off while they were still tying
everyone up. It sounded like it came from outside.
Someone asked, "What was that?" and Brendan said
it was a warning that they didn't want anyone bother-
ing them. The kids were already so scared they were
20 crying and whimpering. But that bomb just added a
whole other dimension of fear. It was one of the
many moments that night when I was sure we were
all going to die.

Beth Bender

25 It was awful. They made us crawl on our stomachs
into the center of the gym. The floor was dusty and
you had to put your face on it. Then one of them kept

---

1 **bulked up:** stark ausgeprägt.   4 **wiggle room:** Bewegungsfrei-
heit.   20 **to whimper:** wimmern.

an eye on us while the other made some of the girls
get up and go sit with their backs to the doors. I
wasn't surprised they picked girls. They wouldn't have
dared let boys stand up.

Deirdre Bunson

They were talking about what they were going to do
with Sam. And they were talking loud because they
wanted everyone to hear. They wanted him to roll
over on his back so they could shoot him in the knee.
They didn't want to shoot him in the back of the
knee, because they weren't sure if that would cripple
him or not. They wanted to shoot him in the kneecap.
They wanted to make sure he'd be ruined for life.

Paul Burns

They kept kicking me in the head and the arms and
ribs. My hands were tied behind my back, and there
was nothing I could do. It hurt worse than anything
that ever happened on a football field. They wanted
me to roll over so they could shoot me in the knee. I
just didn't want to give in. All I could think about was
next year's football season. It couldn't end this way. It
just couldn't.

Sam Flach

Try to picture this: fifty or sixty kids lying facedown
on that hard gym floor with their hands tied behind
their back. Crying, whimpering, blubbering, calling
out for mercy, pleading to be let go. It was like these

---

11 **to cripple:** verkrüppeln.   12 **kneecap:** Kniescheibe.   26 **to blub-
ber:** heulen.

guys were hunters and we were a bunch of seals, and they were trying to decide which ones to slaughter first.

Dustin Williams

5 I've been a hunter and gun collector all my life, as well as a dues-paying member of the National Rifle Association for close to thirty years. But when I think that it was my guns that those boys used. That those were my bullets they fired. ... Sure, you can say that if
10 they hadn't stolen them from me, they would have stolen them from someone else, but they didn't. Those were my guns. And now I have to live with that.

Jack Phillips

15 It was hard for me to keep an eye on both of them, but each time I thought they weren't looking, I'd try to work my hands free. I was pretty sure I could get them loose.

Paul Burns

---

20 "The day of the shootings [in Oregon], the *Eugene Register-Guard* featured a homey little human-interest piece about the wonderful benefits of firearm education."

Rolling Stone, 7/9/98

---

2 **to slaughter:** abschlachten.   6 **dues-paying:** Beiträge zahlend.
[Subtext]   20 **"Eugene Register-Guard":** Zeitung aus Eugene (Oregon); wörtl. etwa: Archivwächter.   21 **to feature:** (Artikel) bringen.   **homey:** hier: gefühlvoll.

[The bullet wound] hurt like the dickens. I kept expecting to black out or taste blood in my mouth, but strangely, other than the pain, I felt okay.

Allen Curry

5 You couldn't see much. You'd try to lift your head and look around, but after a while your neck muscles would go into spasms and you'd have to put your head back down on that disgusting floor.

Deirdre Bunson

10 They shot Sam in both knees. You heard the shots and you heard Sam scream. Some of the teachers started shouting, but they were drowned out by more shots, and the sound of the bullets ricocheting all over the ceiling again and more lights shattering. Gary and
15 Brendan yelled at the teachers to shut up. They weren't just out to get the jocks. They were out to get everyone.

Dustin Williams

I was lying a few feet from Deirdre. She went nuts
20 when they shot Sam in the knees. I really believe she stopped caring about herself. She screamed at Bren-

---

Before 1980 one medical center in Los Angeles had never admitted a single child for gunshot wounds. From 1980 to 1987 the center admitted thirty-four.

---

1 **like the dickens:** wie der Teufel, furchtbar, unheimlich. 2 **to black out:** ohnmächtig werden. 7 **spasm:** Krampf. 8 **disgusting:** widerlich.

dan and called him a bastard. She called him a scared
little worm and dared him to put down the gun. She
went, "Then we'll see how tough you are."

Everyone tried to lift their head to see. I saw Bren-
5 dan step toward her. Deirdre stopped talking. He knelt
down and pressed the barrel of the gun against her
cheek. She cried out and jerked away. I think the barrel
was hot, and it must have burned her face.

I remember what he said: "Hey, cheerleader, think
10 I give a crap about whether you think I'm tough or not?
I already know I'm not tough. You want to know how
I know? Because you and your A-hole friends have
reminded me every single day since I moved here."

He pressed the barrel of the gun right into the back
15 of her neck. It was really sadistic. Deirdre started to
whimper and begged him not to shoot her. Gary came
over and said something about Deirdre having an accident. They both started to laugh. One of the teachers –
Mr. Flanagan, I think – yelled at them, and they fired
20 another shot into the gym floor. I felt the vibration
against my cheek.

Brendan cursed and said he'd missed. Gary pointed
out that he may have missed, but he'd made a nice hole
in the wood.

25   *Paul Burns*

After the autopsies, the newspapers said they hadn't
been on drugs, but if you ask me, they were acting
like totally whacked-out maniacs. They ran around

---

7 **to jerk away:** zurückzucken.   26 **autopsy:** Autopsie, Leichen-
schau.   28 **whacked-out:** kaputt, übergeschnappt.   **maniac:** Wahn-
sinnige(r).

laughing and shooting up the gym floor. You could hear the wood cracking and splintering. I just kept praying they'd run out of ammunition.

Dustin Williams

5 It was so scary when they started shooting at the floor. You just felt like they were completely psycho. They stopped because they heard my cell phone ring. My mom made me take it to the dance, and I gave it to Dustin to hold. Brendan went over and took it out
10 of Dustin's pocket.

They told you what he said, didn't they? She asked if I was there, and Brendan said yes, but I couldn't come to the phone just then. So my mom asked if I would call her back, and he said he doubted it because I'd prob-
15 ably be dead.

Chelsea Baker

It was sick. I mean, the way they played with everyone's heads. And that thing with the phone and Chelsea Baker's mom ... I don't know, it was just com-
20 pletely sick.

Paul Burns

"'I know some of the guns going out of [my company] end up killing people. ... But I'm not responsible for that.'"

Carlos Garcia, whose semiautomatic TEC-9 is "a gun of choice
25 among drug dealers and drive-by shooters," *People*, 1/10/94

---

2 **to splinter:** (zer)splittern.
[Subtext] 25 **drive-by shooter:** jd., der aus einem fahrenden Auto schießt.

125

Sam [Flach] was sobbing and making these horrible, bloodcurdling moans. Someone yelled out that if they didn't get him help, he might bleed to death. And one of those boys smirked and said, "You think?" That's exactly what they wanted. They wanted him to die a slow, wretched death.

Deirdre Bunson

I heard a metallic clacking and clicking sound. At first I didn't know what it was. I couldn't bend around enough to see. Then I realized it was Brendan and Gary reloading.

Beth Bender

I heard them reloading and looked over at Beth [Bender]. She gave me a miserable look. We'd both realized the same thing: These boys were well armed. They weren't going to run out of bullets anytime soon.

Dick Flanagan

Just because someone owns a gun, or likes to hunt or compete in shooting events, does not make him a so-called gun nut. Many people I know own hunting rifles and shotguns, and handguns for self-protection. I can tell you, however, that privately many of us are opposed to semiautomatics. The problem is that once the gun control people get semiautomatics banned, they will go after handguns. And once those are

---

1 **to sob:** schluchzen.   2 **bloodcurdling:** Grauen erregend.   4 **to smirk:** süffisant grinsen.   8 **clacking:** Klappern.   21 **gun nut:** Schusswaffennarr.

banned, do you know what will happen? Some nut will get ahold of a hunting rifle and kill a bunch of people. The gun control people will use that incident as an excuse to go after hunting rifles.

5
Allen Curry

The police got the idea of using the loudspeaker system. We heard a voice come out of nowhere. It really took everyone by surprise, and they handled it very badly. Instead of trying to reason with the boys, they
10 came on very threatening. Laying out what laws they'd broken and what the consequences would be, and how the longer they waited to lay down their weapons, the worse it would be for them.

I remember trying very hard to imagine what those
15 boys were thinking now. And I thought, *Oh, my God, it's too late. They're armed. They're shooting. They've already wounded people. They've taken hostages. They've broken all these laws already. Real laws. Not baby don't-smoke-in-school laws. If they walk out of*
20 *here alive, they are going to go to jail for a long time. And we all know about that, don't we? What they do to you in there. These poor, crazy boys. Maybe the jocks have tormented them here, but it will be a thousand times worse in jail.*

---

25 Police estimated that Klebold and Harris fired close to nine hundred rounds during the siege at Columbine.

---

2 **to get ahold of s.th.:** etwas in die Hand bekommen. 10 **to lay out:** darlegen, erklären.
[Subtext] 26 **siege:** Belagerung.

And that's when I had an epiphany. Can't you see why they were doing it? They had no protection. They couldn't get away from the bullies and tormentors. Not here, not in jail, not anywhere. So why not kill them? Why not kill themselves? What difference would it make either way?

Beth Bender

They started shooting at the ceiling. I assume they were trying to shoot out the speakers. The police shut down the electricity. You can understand why they did it, but when the gym went dark, it just made everything that much worse.

Dick Flanagan

It went dark, and everyone on the floor just started crying and whimpering even more. It was really pathetic. Brendan and Gary turned on their flashlights. I was scared too. I didn't think they'd shoot me, but I was afraid I might get killed if they blew up the gym

---

In 1992 the District of Columbia adopted a law making gun manufacturers liable for gun deaths. A number of semiautomatic weapons were specifically named in the measure. Several companies simply changed the names of the weapons and continued selling them.

---

1 **epiphany:** Eingebung, Erleuchtung. 3 **bully:** Schlägertyp. **tormentor:** Peiniger(in). 9 **speaker:** *loudspeaker.* 15 f. **pathetic:** herzergreifend, Mitleid erregend.
[Subtext] 19 **District of Columbia:** Verwaltungsbezirk Washington. 20 **liable:** haftbar.

or if the police tried to storm in. And as much as I hated Sam Flach, you just can't let people suffer like that. So when it went dark, I yelled out to Gary that I was there.

Allison Findley

As soon as it went dark, kids started inching away from the center of the gym. Those guys would sweep the flashlights over us, and it was like a bunch of giant inchworms crawling around. They yelled at us not to move and went around making sure [the ones who'd moved] went back. That's when I really got to work trying to get my hands free.

Paul Burns

It was dark. I don't know why, but it reminded me of that scene at the end of *Titanic* where they're all floating in the icy water, just trying to hold on for dear life. They kept sweeping their flashlights around, keeping an eye on everyone. So you'd see those silhouettes of people lying there. Just like in the movie, people were

---

20 Nationwide in 1996 more than six thousand students were expelled for bringing guns to school.

---

6 **to inch away:** sich zentimeterweise wegbewegen, wegkriechen. 8 **giant:** riesig. 9 **inchworm:** Larve eines Falters aus der Familie der Geometridae. 15 **"Titanic":** Anspielung auf den Film aus dem Jahr 1997 mit Leonardo DiCaprio und Kate Winslet in den Hauptrollen. Die »Titanic« stieß 1912 bei ihrer Jungfernfahrt mit einem Eisberg zusammen und sank. Mehr als 1500 Menschen kamen dabei ums Leben.
[Subtext] 20f. **to expel s.o.:** jdn. (von der Schule) verweisen.

crying out for their loved ones and sobbing. It was
really eerie.

Chelsea Baker

[Later] I told the detectives that the boys appeared to
5 be caught off guard when Allison called out in the
dark. Those flashlight beams started swinging around
wildly and then focused on the refreshment table. Allison was standing there. She held her hands up and
squinted in the lights. When the boys saw her, Bren-
10 dan seemed amused. He may have even said something like, "Whoa, this is one strange twist." But Gary
kept asking her what she was doing there. He was
quite upset.

Beth Bender

15 Look, who's kidding who? I was scared to death, but
when I heard Gary asking Allison why she was there,
it scared me even more. You could tell that he ex-
pected something really bad to happen, and he didn't
want her to be part of it.
20

Dustin Williams

When Allison said she thought they should do something to help Sam, the kids became extremely agitated. Up to that point you didn't know whose side
she was on.
25

Dick Flanagan

---

2 **eerie:** gespenstisch, unheimlich. 5 **to be caught off guard:** unvor-
bereitet erwischt werden. 9 **to squint:** die Augen zusammenkneifen,
blinzeln. 11 **twist:** Wendung. 22 f. **agitated:** aufgeregt.

It was a madhouse. I mean, twenty people started yelling at Allison at once. I guess they thought she could reason with those guys. Get them to give up or something.

Paul Burns

Brendan started yelling at everyone to shut up, and there was a burst of gunfire. It was insane in the dark. You heard gunfire and had no idea who it was. Was it the police? Those guys? Someone else? And then in the middle of it that girl screamed.

Dustin Williams

I was right next to Robin [Lewis], so when she screamed, I thought they'd shot her. Brendan was yelling at everyone to shut up, but the wailing and crying just tripled. It was beyond nightmarish.

Beth Bender

In 1995 more than one million guns manufactured outside the United States were imported into this country. More than half were handguns.

---

1 **madhouse:** Irrenhaus. 14 **wailing:** Gejammer. 15 **to triple:** sich verdreifachen.

131

Brendan's Suicide Note

To the good people of Middletown:

I hope this gets printed in big, bold letters on the front page of the newspaper, because it's something every single one of you should read. I'm gone now, and you want to know why I took your kids with me?

Here's why. You made my friggin' life miserable. How? By the way you raised your kids to all want to be the same and to hate anyone who dares to be a little different. Oh, no, you're probably thinking, you didn't do that.

You sure did. I've seen you in your cars staring at me and my friends. *Look at those creeps. Look at their clothes and the music they listen to. Why can't they go out for sports or at least root for our team?*

Know what? Not everybody has to do what you A-holes want them to do. Maybe your kids did, but me and my friends chose not to. And you and your kids couldn't deal with that. And so you had to do what stupid, ignorant people always do when they don't understand – you had to attack and torment us.

And you teachers. I thought you taught us that America is supposed to be about freedom. Kids are supposed to be able to be different without the status quo police smashing us over the head and ridiculing us. But that's all you teachers did to me and my friends. Just like everyone else, you tried to make us conform to your narrow-minded expectations of how we were supposed to dress and act.

Well, screw you. Screw all of you. I hope this letter is like a knife in your hearts. You ruined my life. All I've done is pay you back in kind.

Respectfully yours,
5   Brendan Lawlor

4 **Respectfully yours:** etwa: Hochachtungsvoll.

The End

Brendan started to shoot again. From the muzzle
flashes I knew he was firing at the ceiling. But in the
dark like that a lot of kids couldn't see and didn't
5 know. They just assumed everyone around them was
being slaughtered. You don't know what terror really
is until you experience it yourself.

Dustin Williams

Robin [Lewis] screamed because she felt warm liquid
10 seeping into her clothes from the floor and thought it
was blood. Everyone knows now it was something
else. It's just completely gross.

Deirdre Bunson

You lose track of how many times you think this is it,
15 you're really going to die now, but that was certainly
one of those moments. Brendan was screaming at
everyone to shut up. He probably fired that semiautomatic until he'd emptied the whole clip. There were
bullets ricocheting all over the place. A couple of kids
20 were grazed. We're incredibly lucky no one was actually hit. It was utter mayhem.

Allen Curry

---

2 f. **muzzle flash:** Mündungsfeuer.   10 **to seep:** sickern.   20 **to graze
s.o.:** jdn. streifen.

It got quiet, and I heard those clicking sounds and realized Brendan was reloading. Then I heard Gary say, "Brendan, we gotta talk." Brendan cursed him out something awful. So now *these* two guys were ar-
5 guing. I guess it was something in Gary's voice. Everyone who heard it started begging Brendan to listen to him. Of course, that just totally set Brendan off again.

Chelsea Baker

10 In a situation like that, you search madly for anything to hope for. When I heard Gary say they had to talk, I thought we had a chance. It wasn't much, but it was all we had. But with all the crying and pleading, Brendan wasn't listening. So I raised my voice and told
15 everyone to quiet down and let the boys talk.

Beth Bender

First Brendan was screaming at everyone to shut up. Then Ms. Bender said we should be quiet. Then Mr. Flanagan said it too. It was so weird. They were all
20 agreeing with Brendan. For a second I thought they'd gone over to the other side or something.

Deirdre Bunson

Like any other business, the gun industry must constantly intro-
duce new products to keep buyers interested and enhance profits.
25 People who buy computers look for more memory and faster chip
speed. People who buy guns look for increased killing power.

---

3 f. **to curse s.o. out:** jdn. beschimpfen.
[Subtext] 25 **memory:** Speicher(kapazität). 25 f. **chip speed:** Pro-
zessorgeschwindigkeit.

Everyone [on the floor] started whispering to each other to be quiet and let [the boys] talk. In the dark I heard Brendan say he couldn't effing believe it. He just couldn't effing believe it.

Allison Findley

Gary wanted to talk. Brendan said there was nothing to talk about. They'd chosen their path. So Gary goes, "Things have changed." Brendan started cursing at him and saying nothing had changed. The rest of us just lay there listening to it. Here were these two crazy boys discussing whether we'd live or not. Our lives were totally in their hands.

Chelsea Baker

I worked my hands free. If there'd just been one [guy with a gun], I think I would have jumped up in the dark and taken him down. But there were two. I thought about grabbing one, getting his gun, and shooting the other, but it seemed awful risky. The truth is I was brought up in a family that was totally

---

Several studies have pointed out that the number of rampage shootings each year has remained somewhat consistent. However, the number of victims has increased dramatically. The reason? Semiautomatic weapons capable of spraying more bullets in a shorter period of time.

---

4 **effing:** euphemistisch für *fucking*.
[Subtext] 20 f. **rampage shooting:** blindwütige Schießerei, Amoklauf. 21 **consistent:** gleichbleibend.

against guns and I'd never actually fired one. I wasn't
sure I'd know how.

Paul Burns

Gary said he was still with Brendan all the way, but
5 they had to get Allison out of there. Brendan was
completely sarcastic. Like, exactly how did Gary pro-
pose to do that? You know, with the doors locked and
booby-trapped. Meanwhile, I started to hear this
strange sound. Something half whirring, half grinding.
10 I realized it was a drill. Someone was trying to drill
into the gym.

Dustin Williams

They both stopped talking. I heard the drilling sound
and knew they were listening too. They started swing-
15 ing their flashlights over the walls and the basketball
nets and the air-conditioning ducts, trying to see
where the sound was coming from. I heard a screech
of metal and looked up. Of course, it was pitch-black
and I couldn't see anything. Those boys were swing-
20 ing their flashlights around like spotlights at a movie
premiere. Then one of the beams fixed on something.
It was a black cable wire coming down from the ceiling. Near the end it curved slightly, and something at
the very end of it reflected the light from the flash-
25 light beam: I thought, *Well, what do you know? It's a
camera*.

Dick Flanagan

---

4 **to be with s.o. all the way:** mit jdm. ganz einig sein.   9 **to whirr:** sur-
ren, brummen.   **to grind:** mahlen.   10 **drill:** Bohrer.   17 **screech:**
Knirschen.   18 **pitch-black:** pechschwarz, völlig dunkel.   25 **what
do you know?:** etwa: stell dir bloß vor!

This was unreal. No one's saying anything. Except for the flashlights it's still dark. In the flashlight beam you can see this wire thing slowly start to turn in a circle. Like it's looking around to see what the story is.

5
Paul Burns

I rolled onto my side a little so I could see what everyone was looking at. It was hard to see the cable, because if the flashlight beam moved just a little, you lost sight of it. Then out of nowhere there's this voice
10 whispering in my ear. It was Paul, and he said he'd gotten his hands free.

Dustin Williams

I was so glad when I saw that camera come down. So they'd know Brendan and Gary had put us near the
15 doors, and if anyone tried to come in, those doors might explode.

Chelsea Baker

I have a key ring with a nail clipper on it. It was in the front pocket of my pants. I told Paul to put his hand
20 in my pocket and get it. So Paul put his hand in my pocket and, of course, that's exactly when the lights started to go back on.

Dustin Wiliams

"'We are focusing on dollars more than anything else. ... For us, a
25 great deal of the motivation is to run a profitable company.'"

A former president of Smith & Wesson, *Making a Killing*

---

18 **nail clipper:** Nagelknipser.
[Subtext]   26 **president:** (Aufsichtsrats- und) Vorstandsvorsitzende(r).

138

You heard that hum, and the lights that weren't shot
out started to glow a little. It took a few minutes. I
knew Sam was somewhere near me, so I squirmed
around until I could see him. He was pale, and his
face was a grimace of pain. From the thighs down his
pant legs were soaked with blood, and there were
dark red puddles on the floor. I'm not a medical professional, but I sensed it was only a matter of time
until he bled to death.

Beth Bender

[When the lights went on,] Paul's first reaction was to
pull his hand out of my pocket. I whispered, "No, get
the nail clipper!" He did. Gary and Brendan were so
busy looking at the TV camera, they never saw. We
were really lucky.

Dustin Williams

After the lights went back on, they dropped a thinner
black wire through the hole. At the end of it was a
little, round black thing. It was about the size of one
of those microphones you can clip to your collar.
Then they turned the gym speakers back on, and this
calm voice said, "Brendan? Gary?" Brendan started
firing at that tiny microphone. You could tell he didn't
like what was happening.

Deirdre Bunson

It wasn't the same person [on the loudspeaker] as before. This guy was really calm and professional. He

---

1 **hum:** Summen, Brummen.   5 **grimace:** Grimasse.   **thigh:** Ober-
schenkel.   6 **soaked:** durchtränkt.

told Brendan and Gary that even if they managed to
hit the mike and put it out of commission, they'd just
send down another one. At first Brendan was fit to be
tied, but then he calmed down. I guess he figured out
5 that he was still in control.

Dustin Williams

Brendan's mom and dad got on the speaker. It was
really pitiful. His mom was crying. His dad sounded
like he was in agony. They both pleaded with him to
10 stop and give up. They talked about how much they
loved him and wanted to help him and how wrong it
was to hurt other people and why hadn't he told them
how stressed he was? I couldn't see his face because
of the mask. But I really wished I could.

15

Chelsea Baker

They put on Gary's mom next. She tried to talk, but
her voice cracked and she just started to bawl. Then
the negotiator guy comes back on and starts talking
about how they're not just hurting the people in the

---

20 "'The big thing about firearms is that they do give the weak a way
to defend themselves against the strong.'"

William Ruger Sr., president of Ruger, a manufacturer of
semiautomatic weapons, *Making a Killing*

---

2 **mike:** Kurzform von *microphone*.　**to put s.th. out of commission:**
etwas außer Funktion setzen.　3f. **to be fit to be tied:** etwa: völlig
durchdrehen.　17 **to bawl:** heulen.　18 **negotiator:** Unterhändler,
Vermittler.
[Subtext]　22 **Ruger:** bekannter amerikanischer Schusswaffenhersteller.

gym, they're hurting their families, too. They're de-
stroying their parents' lives. Brendan walked over to
Sam Flach, who was still lying there bleeding. He
looks up at the little camera and asks if the negotiator
5 guy can see him. The cable turned a little, and the guy
said yes. Brendan asked if they could see all the blood
seeping out of Sam's knees, and the negotiator said
yes. Brendan knelt down and put the barrel of his gun
right next to Sam's ear and said that if they didn't re-
10 move that camera and mike right now, he would put a
bullet in Sam's head. The next thing we knew, the
camera and microphone started to rise back up to the
ceiling.

Allison Findley

15 Paul had the nail clippers, but with the lights on,
Brendan and Gary could see us. I was praying to God
as hard as I could that the lights would go off again.

Dustin Williams

I'm not sure I believe in miracles, but ever since that
20 night, I definitely believe in angels. Only you never
know who they might be or what form they might
take. If Allison Findley could be an angel, anyone
could.

Dick Flanagan

25 I heard a really horrible groan. Allison was kneeling
over Sam, and at first I thought she was torturing him
or something. But she'd taken off her belt and put it

---

25 **groan:** Stöhnen.

141

around one of Sam's thighs and was tightening it like
a tourniquet. Brendan yelled at her to get away from
Sam. Allison said no without even looking at him.
Brendan came over and said he'd kill her if she didn't
5 leave Sam alone. Allison looked up at him and said,
"Know what, Brendan? I know you don't care about
living. Well, neither do I. Go ahead and kill me."
Maybe she knew Brendan wouldn't shoot her. Maybe
she truly didn't care.
10
Chelsea Baker

Paul and I weren't that far from Sam. Allison used
her belt to try and stop the bleeding in one of his legs,
and then she started to look around for another belt.
So naturally she looked at guys. Paul had his hands
15 behind him, like he was pretending they were still
tied. He had the nail clipper in his fist. Allison walked
over to us and looked down at him. My heart was
beating so hard I thought I was going to puke.
Dustin Williams

20 Brendan and Gary were standing shoulder to
shoulder, arguing. One faced one way, the other faced
the other way. So they were each watching 180 de-
grees of the room. I assumed they were fighting about
Allison. At first I didn't quite grasp it. What was the
25 big deal? Why did they care if she stayed? Just because she was there didn't necessarily mean she'd
have to come to harm, did it? Not unless they were
planning to kill everyone … including themselves.
Beth Bender

2 **tourniquet:** Binde, Aderpresse.   18 **to puke:** kotzen.

142

Allison bent over Paul. I saw her look down at him,
then kind of blink and straighten up. I thought, *This is
it. Good-bye, world. I hope Heaven's exactly the same
way they pictured it in that* South Park *movie.*

Dustin Williams

It wasn't really an argument. It was Brendan yelling
at Gary about what they'd agreed on and how hard
they'd worked, and how if they didn't do this, nothing
would ever change. And Gary looking like he had a
headache, closing his eyes and pressing his fingers
against his temple and saying over and over again, "I
know, I know, I know." And I kept thinking, what had
they worked so hard for? And you knew it was this.
The planning and the booby-trapping and the bombs,
and I couldn't help imagining the effort that must
have gone into it. What an enormous force it must
have been that twisted these boys' minds to the point
that they would work so hard to do this.

Beth Bender

[Allison] was standing right over me. I started saying
good-bye to everyone. I mean, in my head. I guess I

"The ultimate fact is that the gun industry is simply a business. …
The people who make, import and sell guns … are businessmen.
They want to make money, and as much of it as possible."

Making a Killing

---

2 **to blink:** blinzeln. **to straighten up:** sich aufrichten. 4 **"South
Park":** umstrittene populäre Trickfilmserie (seit 1997), in der das Bild
des Himmels stark sexuell geprägt ist.

143

closed my eyes, because when I opened them Allison was still staring at me.

Paul Burns

The Lord says we should do unto others as we would
5 have them do unto us. It's not very complicated.

Chelsea Baker

[Allison] walked away. For a second I thought she was going to tell Brendan and Gary. But she knelt down next to Joey Graves and told him she was going
10 to undo his belt. Can you believe Joey? He actually said he'd always dreamed of that. Allison said, "Don't be an A-hole."

Paul Burns

The way I heard it, she took Joey's belt and went over
15 to Sam and did the same thing she'd done to his other leg. You know, the doctor said if she hadn't done that, he probably would have bled to death. The thing is, can you picture that? Allison Findley saving Sam Flach's life?
20

Ryan Clancy

"Time and time again, the gun industry has injected into the civilian market new guns that are specifically designed to be better at killing."

Making a Killing

[Subtext]   21 **time and time again:** immer wieder.   **to inject:** einführen, bringen.

Brendan went ballistic on Gary. He yanked off his
mask and threw it on the floor. And Gary, I don't
know, he just shut down. He walked over to the wall,
sat down, and buried his head in his arms. Now Bren-
5 dan's storming around, yelling great, just effing great!
Neither of them was paying attention to anything.
Dustin nudged me with his foot, and I rolled around
and clipped the tie holding his hands.

Paul Burns

10 It sounded like a firecracker. Everyone was looking
around like, *What was that?* Allison screamed out
Gary's name. He was lying on his side. It was horrible.

Chelsea Baker

I wanted more guys, but when Gary shot himself, I
15 didn't know what was going to happen next. Allison
went running to Gary. Brendan followed her, but he
was walking. He had his back to us. We do up-downs
in football. That's where we drop to our stomach,
then jump back up. The coaches are always on me be-
20 cause I'm not the fastest to get up, but I was then.

I knew Brendan was going to hear me coming. I was
just hoping he wouldn't have time to turn around, aim,
and fire.

Dustin Williams

25 It didn't seem real. That little popping noise, and then
Gary slumped over and the blood started to run out

---

7 **to nudge:** (leicht) anstoßen.   8 **to clip:** durchtrennen.   25 **to pop:**
knallen.   26 **to slump over:** vornüber zusammensacken.

of his head. His arms and legs started jerking. It was just so gross. I kept thinking, *No way. This is a dream. It's a movie.*

                                                            Deirdre Bunson

5 [Brendan] heard my footsteps and started to turn with the gun, but I tackled him as hard as I could and slammed him down against the gym floor. That #$*%ing gun slid away, and I held Brendan down. He struggled and cursed a lot, but that was it.

10   *Dustin Williams*

Dustin Williams is a hero. There's no doubt about that.

                                                            Allen Curry

They say Dustin's a hero, but I don't believe he was
15 trying to be one. I think he was only doing what he knew had to be done. Something bad was going on, and he had to stop it. It's what a moral human being is supposed to do.

                                                            Chelsea Baker

20 We all saw what happened. Suddenly every kid was screaming for Paul to free them. Can you blame

---

More American children are killed by firearms than by all natural causes combined.

---

6 **to tackle:** angreifen, packen.   7 **to slam:** schlagen, knallen.

them? We all wanted to get out of there. That's when
I remembered the doors were booby-trapped.

Beth Bender

It was complete hysteria. Paul was going around with
those clippers, cutting the ties as fast as he could.
Someone else found a pair of nail clippers, and one of
the boys had a penknife. The kids were crying and
shrieking to be freed next. That little eye-in-the-sky
camera must have been watching the whole time, because the loudspeaker started blaring. But it was lost
in the din. Someone started shouting to stay away
from the doors, but not everyone was paying attention.

Dick Flanagan

I was holding Brendan down. He was cursing and crying and squirming. I'm not going to name names, but
someone grabbed me from behind and yanked me
off. At least six other guys were on him in no time.

Dustin Williams

I tried to get up, but I couldn't. The slightest move-
ment and the pain was overwhelming. It's not like the
movies. At least it wasn't for me. You don't get hit
and keep going. You get shot and you go down and
stay there.

Allen Curry

---

7 **penknife:** Taschenmesser.   8 **to shriek:** kreischen.   **eye-in-the-
sky:** Decken-.   10 **to blare:** plärren.   11 **din:** Krach, Lärm.

At that point I wasn't thinking about Brendan. I was thinking about the kids who were heading for the doors. They were chained shut, but we knew they were booby-trapped. We had to make sure those kids stayed away from the doors. We had no idea how much or how little it might take to make one blow.

Dick Flanagan

Dustin was holding Brendan. I don't think Brendan was going to escape. Those boys got free, and the first thing on their minds was to get Brendan. I still don't understand what they were thinking.

Chelsea Baker

You had four exits. You ran to one, and if there was already someone there trying to keep the kids from pulling on the doors, you ran to the next [set of doors] and tried to stop those kids. Some of them understood, but some of them were panicked and irrational. To be honest, I wasn't really aware of what else was going on.

Dick Flanagan

In 1997, after a man armed with handguns killed sixteen children and a teacher at Dunblane Primary School in Scotland, Britain banned all handguns.

[Subtext]   23 **Dunblane:** schottische Kleinstadt nahe Stirling, in der am 13. 3. 1996 Thomas Hamilton in einer Grundschule siebzehn Menschen erschoss und danach Selbstmord beging.

148

They wanted to kill him. The way they were stomping on his head, it was sickening. He wasn't even conscious. Just limp like a doll.

Dustin Williams

5 I tried to stop them. I was the only one. One of them cursed me out and pushed me away. Then I went to get Ms. Bender. She was telling kids to stay away from the doors. I told her they were killing Brendan. She told me to keep everyone away from the doors
10 and ran over there.

Allison Findley

What Brendan and Gary did was terribly, horribly, inexcusably wrong. I have no interest in defending them. But deep in my heart there's a little piece of me
15 that at least understands what might have driven them to such a horrendous, evil undertaking. But what those boys did was equally inexcusable and evil.

Beth Bender

"After thirty-five people were killed by a gunman with an array of
20 assault weapons … in 1996, Australia banned all automatic and semiautomatic weapons and pump-action shotguns, paid their owners a fair price, and destroyed the lot."

Making a Killing

---

1 **to stomp:** trampeln, treten.   3 **limp:** schlaff.   12f. **inexcusably**
(adv.): unentschuldbar, unverzeihlich.   16 **horrendous:** entsetzlich.
[Subtext]   19 **array:** Sammlung, Arsenal.   21 **pump-action shotgun:**
Pumpgun, Repetiergewehr.   22 **the lot:** alle(s).

I didn't try to stop [the boys beating Brendan]. I guess at that point I was just so wiped out and stressed that I didn't care. I know those guys have to be punished. The police have already told my parents
5 I'll have to testify about what I saw. This may sound terrible, but I still wonder, if I had to do it again, would I try to stop them next time? And I don't know what the answer is.

Dustin Williams

10 Everyone is convinced that Brendan and Gary would have let Sam die, and would have killed many more. Maybe they're right. Maybe not. The fact is the only person Gary killed was himself. And Brendan didn't kill anyone. I know he shot Sam und Mr. Curry, but
15 maybe [Brendan and Gary] would have changed their minds and let everyone live. Maybe they would have let Sam bleed a little longer and then gotten him help. No one will ever know. But this much I do know: The only people I saw really try to kill anyone
20 that night were those boys. They tried to kill Brendan with their bare hands. And I am absolutely convinced that if it hadn't been for Ms. Bender, they would have.

Allison Findley

25 I speak to Mrs. Lawlor about once a week. Brendan is still in a coma. The doctors say his brain damage is irreversible. The courts will have to decide whether

---

2 **wiped out:** völlig leer. 5 **to testify:** (vor der Polizei) aussagen.
27 **irreversible:** nicht umkehrbar, unheilbar.

to disconnect his life support. Apparently there's a group of people somewhere who are against it. Whoever they are, they certainly don't know the Lawlors or anyone else around here. Sometimes I
5 wonder what has happened to the world. How we got to a place where mercy seems so hard to come by.

Beth Bender

You want to know what it was? Pure evil, plain and simple. How else do you explain a boy being as nice
10 and polite as Brendan Lawlor and then doing what he did?

Jack Phillips

I've been awarded a partial scholarship to an Ivy League college back east. Back where all the "liberal
15 gun control" people live. I bet half the newspaper editors who wrote editorials attacking our school went to that kind of college. I had good grades and boards, but I know kids, even African American kids like me, who had better grades and boards and didn't get into
20 one of those schools. Know why I got in? Because I made second-team all-state linebacker. One of those Ivy League teams back east needed a linebacker. Kind of ironic, huh?

Dustin Williams

1 **to disconnect:** ab-, ausschalten.   **life support:** lebenserhaltende Apparate.   13 **partial scholarship:** Teilstipendium.   13 f. **Ivy League:** Sammelbezeichnung für die acht berühmten Universitäten im Nordosten der USA.   16 **editorial:** Leitartikel.   17 **boards** (pl.): Prüfungsergebnisse.   21 **linebacker:** Verteidigungsspieler im American Football, der unmittelbar hinter dem Gedränge steht.

My pastor says I have to try and forgive them for what they did to me. Meanwhile I'm still on crutches with two knees that'll never be any good again. Why? Did I do anything that a thousand other guys at a thousand other schools haven't done? Sorry, folks, I'm not forgiving them. Ever.

Sam Flach

The memory of what happened surrounds me like a cloak of pain. A hundred questions buzz around my head: How did it happen? When did it go from a fantasy to an actual plan? I know I'll never understand what happened in Brendan's mind. But I thought I knew Gary better. What pushed him over the line? How did he get to the point where he just didn't care? What really scares me is when I think about how close I came to that point myself.

From Allison Findley's journal

A schoolteacher's job is to teach, not to raise children. As far as raising children, I raised my three just fine. They are all good, moral young adults, and two of them own guns, which they use for target

---

"'We'll never understand why this tragedy happened, or what we might have done to prevent it. … We did not see anger or hatred in Dylan until the last moments of his life, when we watched in helpless horror with the rest of the world.'"

Dylan Klebold's parents, *New York Times*, 6/29/99

---

2 **crutch:** Krücke.   9 **cloak:** Hülle, Umhang.   **to buzz:** summen, schwirren.

shooting and hunting. If you're looking for answers, you're not going to find them in school. Many people around here believe that, at least in this case, the parents were pretty blameless. I'll be honest with you. I
5 don't know what to think about that. And I don't have any answers.

Dick Flanagan

I've heard the argument that it's okay to give guns to kids as long as you make sure they're trained on how
10 to use them safely. I have to disagree. These are children, and they can be extremely emotional and impulsive and not always completely in touch with reality. The statistics show that guns are now the number one killer of young people in this country.
15 You can train a young man all you want, but if he's just been dumped by his girlfriend, or picked on by someone much bigger and stronger than him … well, I'm just not convinced that all the safety training in the world is going to stop him from grabbing that gun
20 and doing what he thinks he has to do.

Beth Bender

The community has made it clear that they want metal detectors and security guards in school. They want backpacks banned as well. I think it's a shame
25 that we have to resort to these measures, but if that's what the community wants, I'm prepared to comply.

Allen Curry

---

16 **to dump s.o.:** jdn. fallen, sitzen lassen.   23 **metal detector:** Metalldetektor (Gerät zur Entdeckung von Metall).   26 **to comply:** sich beugen, fügen.

There was an article in the newspaper recently about
the NRA paying for programs that promote hunting
and gun use among children. I have nothing against
hunting. My dad hunted, and some of my fondest
5 memories are of sitting around the dinner table eating
venison and hearing his hunting stories. But personally, I think hunting is something parents can teach
their children about, just like my father learned from
his father. I don't understand why a big national or-
10 ganization feels it must spend all this money to make
sure children learn about guns.

Kit Conner

Want to know what a trigger lock is? It's something
you take off a gun and throw away.

Jack Phillips
15

I'm not sure what it will take to change. Everyone
knows that guns and violence are deeply ingrained in
our culture. You've got about as much chance of getting people to give up their guns as you do getting them
20 to give up driving or drinking beer at baseball games.
Innocent victims die because of guns, but they also die
because of car accidents, acts of terrorism, fires, and
food poisoning. We find the idea of kids being killed

Middle school students possessed 853 of the 1,249 weapons
25 found in public schools statewide in Virginia during the 1991–92
school year.

---

2 **NRA:** Abk. für *National Rifle Association.*   6 **venison:** Wild.
13 **trigger lock:** Abzugschloss.

154

in school especially repugnant because we send our children there expecting them to be safe. But it appears that no place is safe anymore.

F. Douglas Ellin

5 I sincerely believe that this tragedy didn't have to happen. Maybe Gary and Brendan were different from other kids, but they still should have been accepted as people. Maybe there should be a mandatory course in school that teaches kids to respect one an-
10 other no matter what. I think that would be a lot more helpful than geometry.

Emily Kirsch

I read in the newspaper that the kind of guns they had are pretty much the same thing the army uses.
15 They're not made for hunting or target practice. They're just made to kill people. Why in the world are stores allowed to sell them?

Chelsea Baker

I used to drive through towns and see signs proclaim-
20 ing, "Drug-Free Zone." Now the signs say, "Gun-Free Zone." But by the time they're thinking about guns,

---

A program for resolving conflicts creatively was tested in New York City public elementary schools. It was found that students in the program tended to be less hostile and were more likely to
25 choose verbal rather than physical strategies to resolve conflicts.

---

1 **repugnant:** abstoßend, widerwärtig.

it's too late. The signs should read, "Teasing/Bullying-Free Zone." My son was different, and he was made to pay for that every day of his short life. Perhaps if we spent as much time teaching tolerance as we do
5 teaching athletics, my son would be alive today.

Cynthia Searle

Even now when I go to school, I know I'm being watched. Ryan and I leave little pieces of paper wedged in the bottom of our locker doors, and about
10 once a week they're gone. We walk down the hall, and teachers stop talking. Nothing's changed. In fact, in some ways it's gotten worse. If you act different or dress different, you're automatically suspect.

Allison Findley

15 In the wild, animals pick on the weaker members of the pack. This is done partly to establish a pecking order and partly to protect the pack against weakness. It is no different with children. Teasing, bullying, fighting – these are how children establish their peck-
20 ing order. It is, unfortunately, natural for children to do this. And it is the responsibility of adults to supervise and stop this behavior. One thing that is wrong with our schools is that we are permitting too much of the former and not enough of the latter.

25 *F. Douglas Ellin*

I think about the stuff we did – fooling around with bombs and guns, drinking and driving – things that

---

1 **to bully:** schikanieren. 9 **to wedge:** hier: verkeilen. 16f. **pecking order:** Hackordnung.

could really kill us. But we didn't know. I swear it was like we were living in some make-believe world. I truly believe that if Gary and Brendan could come back now and see what they did – to themselves and their parents and everyone else – they wouldn't have done it. No one would.

Ryan Clancy

We live in a culture of brutality. People seem to think that it's perfectly acceptable to be violent. Look at

---

"'We have a little moneymaking machine here. All we have to do is keep introducing the correct new products. ... We operate on a philosophy that you have to have new stuff, and you have to have it annually.'"

William Ruger Sr., president of Ruger, a gun company whose semiautomatic handguns were used by Colin Ferguson to kill six and wound nineteen on a Long Island Railroad train, and by Michael Carneal to kill three and wound five in Paducah, Kentucky, *Making a Killing*

"'It's not my fault. It really isn't.'"

The president of a major gun manufacturer, when asked about the gun industry's responsibility for firearms violence, *Making a Killing*

[Subtext] 15 **Ferguson:** Wegen sechsfachen Mordes im Jahre 1993 wurde Colin F. zu sechsmal lebenslänglicher Haft verurteilt. 16 **Long Island:** zum Bundesstaat New York gehörende Insel, auf der die New Yorker Stadtbezirke Brooklyn und Queens liegen.

wrestling on TV. Even when it's fake, we love the savageness of it. Maybe that's the norm outside of school, but I am just plain sorry – when it happens in school, you cannot simply walk away from it and say
5 boys will be boys. It must be stopped.

Beth Bender

---

1 **fake:** unecht; Schwindel.   1 f. **savageness:** Brutalität.

Postscript

I have spent hundreds of hours interviewing, listening, and reading. Even after all that, I still don't know what went on in Gary's mind. Didn't he know there
5 were alternatives? He could have transferred to another school or even dropped out altogether. How did he get to the point where he believed guns and bombs were the only way to solve his problems?

I stand outside Middletown High, the school I gra-
10 duated from just three years ago, and I know I'm a changed person. We all are. In Middletown, in our state, in this country. Around the world. Can anything good come from this? Is any lesson worth this cost? Two lives destroyed at Middletown High School. At
15 other schools, dozens more lives lost. Kids who had as much right to live as any of us, gone. Robbed in moments of absolute insanity.

What I do know is that from now on I will pay attention more carefully – not just to the words and what

---

20 After a school shooting in Canada, the Canadian government spent
$ 1 million to expand programs to combat bullying in schools and
to help students before they get into trouble.

---

6 **to drop out:** (Schule) abbrechen.   17 **insanity:** Wahnsinn.
[Subtext]   21 **to combat:** bekämpfen.

they mean, but to whom they're coming from. I think
we are too often fooled by the outward sophistication
of teenagers. We forget that they are still children, and
that they are impressionable and impulsive and likely
5 to follow the example of adults. If the teachers and administrators at a school are intolerant of differences
between students, then some of the students are likely
to follow their lead.

And if I ever decide to have children, I will make
10 sure they go to a school where civility is taught and
where differences between people are embraced, not
ridiculed. In this country we have raised consciousness
about drunk driving, smoking, and drug use. We can do
the same with respecting others.

15 And the guns. There are millions of people in this
country who own hunting and target weapons and use

"'What made the difference [in my vote]? ... Twelve dead
children, one dead adult, twenty-four injured kids, and a community that has had its heart broken. ...'"
20 Colorado Republican congressman Tom Tancredo, who accepted
a campaign donation from the NRA but voted for gun control
after seeing what happened at Columbine High School.
Congressman Tancredo lives in Littleton, Colorado.
New York Times, 6/21/99

---

2 **sophistication:** Raffiniertheit, Subtilität.   4 **impressionable:** leicht
zu beeindrucken.   10 **civility:** Höflichkeit.   11 **to embrace s.th.:**
etwas annehmen, akzeptieren.
[Subtext]   20 **congressman:** Kongressabgeordneter (Senator oder
Mitglied des Repräsentantenhauses).   **Tom Tancredo:** republikani-
sches Mitglied des Repräsentantenhauses.   21 **donation:** Spende;
Stiftung.

them responsibly. I don't think hunting weapons should be outlawed, but I do believe it is time for compromise. Most semiautomatic weapons serve no purpose other than to kill people. They should be out-
5 lawed. In this time of budget surpluses, the government should pay a fair price for the semiautomatics that already exist and destroy them. Handguns should be in the hands of law enforcement agencies. The sale and importation of ammunition should be strictly regula-
10 ted.

Gary Searle was my stepbrother. He wasn't a monster, just a boy who thought he'd run out of options. He was part of my life. I loved him; I still do. It is too late to help him, but we all know others like him. I will try to
15 help them. And maybe, after reading this story, you will too.

Denise Shipley

---

2 **to outlaw s.th.:** etwas ächten, verbieten.   5 **budget surplus:** Haushaltsüberschuss.   8 **law enforcement agency:** Polizei.

While This Book Was Being Written

7/29/99 – Mark O. Barton kills nine and wounds
twelve in an office in Atlanta. He uses two handguns.

5 8/10/99 – Buford O. Furrow Jr. kills a postal worker
with a Glock handgun and uses an Uzi submachine
gun to wound four children and one adult at the
North Valley Jewish Community Center in Los Angeles.

10 9/15/99 – Larry Gene Ashbrook kills seven people
(including four teens) in church. He uses a 9 mm
semiautomatic Ruger pistol.

10/4/99 – A New York City school principal is
wounded by a student carrying a gun.

15 * 10/11/99 – Under the weight of twenty-eight lawsuits filed by various cities and counties, the Colt
Manufacturing Company announces plans to stop
selling handguns to the public. Sales in the future

---

5 **postal worker:** Postangestellte(r).   6 f. **Uzi submachine gun:** Ma-
schinenpistole aus israelischer Produktion.   15 f. **to file a lawsuit:**
einen Rechtsstreit, Prozess anstrengen.   16 **county:** Verwaltungsbezirk.

will be limited to the military and law enforcement agencies.

* 10/13/99 – New Jersey becomes the fourth state to prohibit the sale of any new handgun unless it is accompanied by a trigger lock.

10/29/99 – South High School in Cleveland is closed and the homecoming dance canceled after officials discover an alleged plan by four students to shoot others. The school was searched and no guns or other weapons were found, prompting some to wonder how serious the plan was. Other students reported that the four were among a group of kids who were considered outcasts and were often picked on.

11/1/99 – A high school in Redmond, Washington, is closed by the administration after threats are made on the Internet to kill everyone at school.

11/2/99 – Byran Uyesugi, age forty, described as a gun enthusiast who owned close to twenty weapons, shoots and kills seven people in an office in Honolulu.

11/19/99 – A thirteen-year-old Denver boy is wounded when a bomb goes off in his bedroom. Authorities say that the boy had been involved in a fight at school several days before.

---

7 **homecoming dance:** Ball zur Feier des Beginns der Football-Saison an amerikanischen Highschools.   8 **alleged:** angeblich.

11/19/99 – Victor Cordova, thirteen, critically wounds a thirteen-year-old classmate in the lobby of their New Mexico middle school. Cordova uses a handgun in the attack.

5 12/6/99 – In Fort Gibson, Oklahoma, a thirteen-year-old boy wounds four classmates. He uses his father's semiautomatic handgun.

12/8/99 – In Veghel, Netherlands, in the first school shooting in the country's history, a seventeen-year-
10 old boy wounds four students and a teacher with a handgun.

12/21/99 – In Oswego, Kansas, five teens are charged with conspiracy to commit murder after their plot to kill students, teachers, and administrators is dis-
15 covered. Police confiscate close to forty weapons from their homes.

12/30/99 – In Tampa, Florida, a man armed with a semiautomatic handgun kills five and wounds three in the lobby and pool area of a Radisson hotel.

20 2/29/00 – In Mount Morris Township, Michigan, six-year-old Kayla Rolland is shot to death in her first-grade classroom by a six-year-old classmate who used a handgun he had found at home.

---

1 **critically** (adv.): (fig.) schwer.   12 f. **to charge s.o. with s.th.:** jdn. wegen einer Sache anklagen.   13 **conspiracy:** Verschwörung, Komplott.   15 **to confiscate:** konfiszieren, beschlagnahmen.

* 3/17/00 – Reacting to lawsuits, Smith & Wesson, the country's biggest handgun manufacturer, agrees to add trigger locks to each new handgun it sells, and to restrictions designed to make it more difficult for
5   criminals to purchase handguns.

* 5/11/00 – In Prairie Grove, Arkansas, a seventh-grade student and a police officer are both wounded from firing at each other after the student was reported walking down a country road with a
10   shotgun. According to police reports, the student had obtained the gun from his home and was returning to school after he was angered by something the principal had said to him.

5/14/00 – Hundreds of thousands of mothers and their
15   families gather in front of the Capitol in Washington, D.C., for the Million Mom March. The event was organized for "common sense" gun control legislation. In addition to licensing and registration, the marchers called for built-in locks on all guns
20   and a ban on military-style assault rifles.

* positive developments

16 **Million Mom March:** 1999 gegründete US-amerikanische Stiftung zur Bekämpfung des Waffengebrauchs durch Jugendliche.

A Partial List of School Shootings

The following list comes from articles in the *Wall Street Journal*, the *New York Times, Rolling Stone*, the *Windsor Star* of Canada, *Time* magazine, the *Rocky Mountain News*, and other sources.

1974 – *Olean, New York*
Anthony Barbaro kills three and wounds nine at his high school.

5/75 – *Centennial Secondary School, Brampton, Ontario, Canada*
Sixteen-year-old Michael Slobodian kills one teacher and one student, and wounds thirteen others, then commits suicide.

10/78 – *Sturgeon Creek Regional Secondary School, Winnipeg, Manitoba, Canada*
A seventeen-year-old student kills a sixteen-year-old student.

2f. **"Wall Street Journal":** amerikanische Wirtschaftszeitung. (Die New Yorker Börse befindet sich in der Wall Street.)   4 **"Windsor Star":** Zeitung aus Windsor im kanadischen Bundesstaat Ontario. **"Time":** wöchentlich erscheinendes amerikanisches Nachrichtenmagazin.   4f. **"Rocky Mountain News":** in Denver (Colorado) erscheinende Tageszeitung.   9 **centennial:** Hundertjahr-, hundertjährig. 14 **creek:** Bach.

1979 – *San Diego, California*
Sixteen-year-old Brenda Spencer uses a rifle given to her as a birthday present to kill two and wound nine at an elementary school near her home.

5 **1985 – *Connecticut***
A thirteen-year-old student opens fire at a junior high school, killing a janitor and wounding two others. He uses a TEC-9 semiautomatic handgun.

12/16/88 – *Atlantic Shores Christian School, Virginia*
10 ***Beach, Virginia***
Sixteen-year-old Nicholas Elliot kills a teacher and a student with a Cobray semiautomatic handgun with multiple thirty-two-round clips.

1/5/93 – *Brentwood High School, Brentwood, New*
15 ***York***
Shooting erupts during a high school basketball game. One student is wounded.

1/18/93 – *East Carter High School, Grayson, Kentucky*
Seventeen-year-old Scott Pennington kills a teacher
20 and a custodian. He uses a handgun.

2/1/93 – *Amityville, New York*
Seventeen-year-old Shem McCoy kills one student and wounds another. He uses a nine-shot .22-caliber semiautomatic handgun.

---

7 **janitor:** Hausmeister(in).   12 **Cobray:** amerikanischer Schusswaffenhersteller.   13 **multiple thirty-two-round clip:** Mehrfachmagazin mit 32 Patronen.   20 **custodian:** Aufseher(in).

10/94 – *Brockton High School, Toronto, Ontario, Canada*

A student allegedly unhappy with his grades shoots two guidance counselors.

10/12/95 – *Blackville, South Carolina*

A sixteen-year-old kills one teacher and wounds another, then kills himself.

10/23/95 – *Redlands, California*

A thirteen-year-old kills one student and wounds another.

11/15/95 – *Richland High School, Lynnville, Tennessee*

Seventeen-year-old Jamie Rouse opens fire with a rifle in a crowded school hallway. He kills one student and one teacher, and wounds one teacher.

2/2/96 – *Frontier Junior High School, Moses Lake, Washington*

Fourteen-year-old honor student Barry Loukaitis kills two students and one teacher, using two guns he took from an unlocked cabinet at home and a .25-caliber semiautomatic pistol from the family car.

2/28/96 – *St. Louis, Missouri*

A teenager is shot to death on a school bus and the driver is wounded. The assailant uses a .38-caliber semiautomatic handgun.

---

4 **guidance counselor:** Beratungslehrer(in), Berater(in). 17 **honor student:** erstklassige(r) Schüler(in).

2/19/97 – *Bethel, Alaska*
Sixteen-year-old Evan Ramsey kills two students and wounds two others with a 12-gauge shotgun left unlocked in his home.

5 10/1/97 – *Pearl High School, Pearl, Mississippi*
Sixteen-year-old Luke Woodham kills his mother, then goes to school and kills two students and wounds seven others.

12/1/97 – *Heath High School, Paducah, Kentucky*
10 Fourteen-year-old Michael Carneal opens fire on an early-morning prayer circle, killing three girls and wounding five other students. He uses a .22-caliber Ruger semiautomatic handgun he had taken, along with two shotguns and two rifles, from
15 a neighbor's house. He carries five hundred rounds of ammunition in his backpack.

12/15/97 – *Stamps High School*
Fourteen-year-old Joseph Todd kills two students.

3/24/98 – *Westside Middle School, Jonesboro, Ar-*
20 *kansas*
Eleven-year-old Andrew Golden and thirteen-year-old Mitchell Johnson kill four students and one teacher, and wound ten others. They arm themselves with three handguns taken from Golden's
25 parents' house, and four handguns and three rifles taken from Golden's grandfather's home, where they were left unlocked.

3 **12-gauge:** Kaliber von 0,12 *inches.*

4/24/98 – *J.W. Parker Middle School, Edinboro, Pennsylvania*

Fourteen-year-old Andrew Jerome Wurst shoots and kills a science teacher and wounds two students and another teacher at an eighth-grade graduation dance. He uses a .25-caliber handgun registered to his father.

5/19/98 – *Lincoln County High School, Fayetteville, Tennessee*

Jacob Davis, an eighteen-year-old honor student, kills a student allegedly dating his ex-girlfriend.

5/21/98 – *Thurston High School, Springfield, Oregon*

Fifteen-year-old Kipland Kinkel kills his parents and then goes to school and kills two students and wounds twenty-two others. He uses a .22-caliber semiautomatic Ruger handgun, a 9 mm Glock handgun, and a Ruger semiautomatic rifle with a fifty-round clip. The rifle was purchased for him by his parents. The handguns were his father's.

6/15/98 – *Armstrong High School, Richmond, Virginia*

Fourteen-year-old student Quinshawn Booker shoots and wounds a basketball coach and a volunteer aide. Another student was the intended victim. He uses a .32-caliber Llama semiautomatic handgun.

---

23 **aide:** Helfer(in). 24 **Llama:** Pistolentyp.

4/20/99 – *Columbine High School, Littleton, Colorado*
Eighteen-year-old Eric Harris and seventeen-year-
old Dylan Klebold kill twelve students and one
teacher and wound twenty-three others, then kill
themselves. They use a TEC-9 semiautomatic handgun, a 9 mm Hi-Point semiautomatic carbine rifle,
and two sawed-off shotguns.

4/28/99 – *W. R. Myers High School, Taber, Alberta,
Canada*
A fourteen-year-old student kills one student and
wounds a second. He uses a .22-caliber rifle.

5/20/99 – *Heritage High School, Conyers, Georgia*
Fifteen-year-old T. J. Solomon wounds six students.
He uses a .22-caliber rifle and a .357-caliber handgun. Both had to be sneaked past a school security
officer and two other security staffers.

2/29/00 – *Mount Morris Township, Michigan*
Six-year-old Kayla Rolland is shot to death by a
six-year-old classmate.

---

6 **Hi-Point:** Markenname des amerikanischen Waffenherstellers
MKS. **carbine rifle:** Karabiner. 7 **sawed-off:** abgesägt. 15 **to
sneak s.th. past s.o.:** etwas an jdm. vorbeischmuggeln. 16 **staffer:**
Mitarbeiter(in).

Final Thoughts

Anyone looking for one simple black-and-white answer to the problem of school violence involving guns will not find it here. Like Beth Bender and Dick Flanagan, I have no one answer. But I do have suggestions: The manufacture, importation, and possession of all semiautomatic assault-type weapons should be banned. The sale of handguns should be restricted to the military and law enforcement agencies. Children should be taught from the earliest age to respect one another's differences. Schools should enact zero tolerance for teasing. Students' achievements off the field should be valued as highly as those on the field.

If these changes are going to occur, they will have to start with you, the young person reading this book. If this story has moved you, then it will be your job to keep these ideas alive, to examine your own life and your own school, to keep these issues in the forefront with open discussions and debate. Mine is the generation that will see true gun reform continually stalled by lobby-fattened politicians. Yours is the generation that may someday have the power to make the real changes that will save young lives.

If you would like to read and explore more about these issues, the following are some valuable resources:

11 **to enact:** praktizieren.   20 **to stall s.th.:** etwas blockieren.
21 **lobby-fattened:** von der Waffenlobby geschmiert, bestochen.

Books

Friday Night Lights, by H.G. Bissinger (Addison-Wesley, 1990), explores the lives of high school football players in a small Texas town and brings to
5   light the conflict between sports and education.

Making a Killing, by Tom Diaz (New Press, 1999), explores the gun industry's efforts to increase profits by constantly introducing deadlier weapons to the gun-buying market, and shows how powerful gun
10   lobbies work to impede the government's efforts to control gun use.

Lethal Passage, by Erik Larson (Crown, 1994), follows the actual history of one semiautomatic, from its creation to the day a sixteen-year-old schoolboy
15   uses it to kill one teacher and severely wound another. Despite being written long before the shootings in Jonesboro, Paducah, and Littleton, the book predicted such incidents.

Magazine Articles

20   Hall, Stephen S., and Adrian Nicole LeBlanc. "The Troubled Life of Boys." *New York Times Magazine*, 22 August 1999.

Labi, Nadya, et al. "Two Boys and Their Guns." *Time*, 6 April 1998.

25   Sullivan, Randall. "A Boy's Life." *Rolling Stone*, 17 September 1998; 1 October 1998.

---

10 **to impede:** behindern.   23 **et al.:** Abk. für *et alii* (Lat.): und andere.

Wilkinson, Peter, and Matt Hendrickson. "Humiliation and Revenge: The Story of Reb and VoDkA." *Rolling Stone*, 10 June 1999.

Other Printed Materials

5 The Violence Policy Center. "Start 'Em Young: Recruitment of Kids into the Gun Culture." April 1999.

The Violence Policy Center. "Young Guns: How the Gun Lobby Nurtures America's Youth Gun Culture." March 1998.

Web Sites

Many of these sites can also provide printed pamphlets and other materials.

www.vpc.org
The Violence Policy Center
Information on guns and youths

www.millionmommarch.com
Million Mom March Foundation
Stopping gun violence

www.pledge.org
Student Pledge Against Gun Violence
Organized to stop violence in schools

5 f. **recruitment:** Rekrutierung, Einführung.   20 **pledge:** Versprechen.

174

www.paxusa.org
Pax
Stopping gun violence

www.gunfree.org
5   *Coalition to Stop Gun Violence*
Stopping gun violence

www.handguncontrol.org
Center to Prevent Handgun Violence
Stopping gun violence

10 **A portion of the money generated from the sale of
this book is being donated to organizations dedicated
to the struggle for gun control.**

---

2 **pax** (Lat.): Frieden.   11 **to donate s.th.:** etwas spenden, stiften.
11 f. (*to be*) **dedicated to s.th.:** sich einer Sache widmen, sich für etwas
einsetzen.

Editorische Notiz

Der englische Text folgt der Ausgabe: Todd Strasser (Pseudonym: Morton Rhue), *Give a Boy a Gun*, New York: Simon Pulse, 2002. Das Glossar erklärt in der Regel alle Wörter, die nicht in *Reclams Englischem Wörterbuch* von Dieter Hamblock (Stuttgart: Reclam, 1996) verzeichnet sind.

Im Glossar verwendete Abkürzungen

adv.	adverb
infml.	informal (umgangssprachlich)
fig.	figuratively (übertragen)
Lat.	Latin
o.s.	oneself
pl.	plural
s.o.	someone
s.th.	something

Literaturhinweise

Borger, Julian, »Ruling Gives Anti-gun Forces a Whiff of Victory«, in: *The Guardian*, 4.1.2002.

Deadly Lessons, Washington: Joseph Henry Press, 2002.

Hurrelmann, Klaus, »Nachwort«, in: Morton Rhue, *Ich knall euch ab*, übers. von Werner Schmitz, Ravensburg: Ravensburger, 2002, S. 146–157.

Klingenstein, Susanne, »Die zweite Welle«, in: *Frankfurter Allgemeine Zeitung*, 8.6.2002.

O'Nan, Stewart, »Sechzehn Opfer plus eins«, in: *Frankfurter Allgemeine Zeitung*, 7.5.2002.

Public Enquiry into the Shootings at Dunblane Primary School 13/3/96, London: The Stationery Office, 1996.

Nachwort

1

Seit dem Massenmord in der schottischen Kleinstadt Dunblane am 13.3.1996, bei dem der 43-jährige Thomas Hamilton sechzehn Erstklässler, deren Lehrerin und dann sich selbst erschoss, hat wohl kein Mordfall in einer Schule die deutsche Bevölkerung so aufgerüttelt wie das Blutbad in Erfurt, bei dem am 26.4.2002 der 18-jährige Schüler Robert Steinhäuser sechzehn Lehrer, einen Schüler und dann sich selbst erschoss. Beide Fälle lösten beispielhafte Solidaritätsaktionen aus – die Webseite der Betroffenen in Schottland existiert auch heute noch – und führten zu erregten Debatten über die Gründe für solche scheinbar unerklärlichen Gräueltaten und zu dem Versuch, rasch geeignete Maßnahmen zu ergreifen, mit denen solche Taten in der Zukunft unmöglich gemacht werden sollten.

Zunächst wurde in beiden Ländern das Waffenrecht verschärft,[1] weil man davon überzeugt war, dass ein erschwerter Zugang zu Schusswaffen einen erheblichen Beitrag zur Lösung des Problems darstellt, wie auch der offizielle Untersuchungsbericht der britischen Regierung nahe legt: »The existence of legally held firearms leads to their use in crime in a significant, though relatively small, number of cases.«[2] Als Beleg für diese These wurden vornehmlich die USA angeführt, in denen 41% aller Haushalte Schusswaffen besitzen und Schusswaffenmorde sechzigmal häufiger sind als in Großbritannien, wo lediglich 4% aller Haushalte eine

---

1 In Großbritannien etwa verboten die Firearms Amendment Acts aus dem Jahr 1997 den Handfeuerwaffenbesitz fast vollständig. 162000 Waffen wurden von der Bevölkerung bei den Polizeidienststellen angeliefert. In Deutschland trat am 1. 4. 2003 ein neues Gesetz mit dem Ziel einer weiteren Verschärfung des Waffenrechts in Kraft.
2 *Public Enquiry into the Shootings at Dunblane Primary School 13/3/96*, Kapitel 9, Abs. 12.

Schusswaffe besitzen.[3] Nicht zuletzt darum wurde auch weltweit den Morden an amerikanischen Schulen[4] in Europa vergleichsweise wenig Aufmerksamkeit geschenkt. In einem Land, so lautete das gängige Argument, wo der ungehinderte Waffenbesitz[5] verfassungsmäßig garantiert sei, wo eine starke Waffenlobby jeden Versuch der Einschränkung des privaten Waffenbesitzes energisch und erfolgreich bekämpfe und wo es eine »spezifisch amerikanische Tradition der Gewalt«[6] gebe, seien solche Untaten eher zu erwarten als in anderen zivilisierten Staaten.

In der Tat lassen sich diese Argumente nicht schlicht vom Tisch wischen. Dennoch ist eine differenziertere Betrachtung angebracht. Zunächst lässt sich nicht bestreiten, dass die Amerikaner »in Sachen Waffengewalt [...] führend auf der Welt sind«,[7] daraus darf aber nicht geschlossen werden, dass derartige Untaten in anderen Ländern allenfalls irrationale, unerklärliche Einzelereignisse sind, während ihnen in den USA ein erklärbares Muster zu Grunde liegt.[8] Gerade Massenmorde an Schulen – und auf diesen Teilaspekt zielen die

3 Interessanterweise liegt die entsprechende Quote für Kanada, wo auch 26% aller Haushalte eine Waffe besitzen, nur bei einem Zehntel des US-amerikanischen Wertes. Die Vergleichszahlen für Deutschland liegen bei 10% und einem Dreißigstel.

4 Allein in den Jahren 1997 bis 1999 kamen in den USA bei vier solchen Fällen zwanzig Menschen ums Leben.

5 Natürlich ist in allen amerikanischen Bundesstaaten Jugendlichen der unbeaufsichtigte Zugang zu Schusswaffen untersagt. Dennoch stellt der Untersuchungsbericht der amerikanischen Akademie der Wissenschaften *Deadly Lessons* (Washington: Joseph Henry Press, 2002) fest, dass die jugendlichen Täter in allen Fällen von Gewaltanwendung an amerikanischen Schulen keinerlei Probleme hatten, sich Waffen zu beschaffen (S. 301).

6 Zit. aus einem Artikel über den vom amerikanischen Kongress beauftragten Untersuchungsbericht des Center for Disease Control and Prevention nach: Susanne Klingenstein, »Die zweite Welle«, in: *Frankfurter Allgemeine Zeitung*, 8.6.2002.

7 Stewart O'Nan, »Sechzehn Opfer plus eins«, in: *Frankfurter Allgemeine Zeitung*, 7.5.2002.

8 Vgl. hierzu Klaus Hurrelmann, »Nachwort«, in: Morton Rhue, *Ich knall euch ab*, übers. von Werner Schmitz, Ravensburg: Ravensburger, 2002, S. 146-157. Hurrelmann setzt sich vor allem mit der Situation an deutschen Schulen auseinander.

folgenden Ausführungen ab – hat man bis vor kurzem vornehmlich mit sozialen Problemgruppen und Rassenfragen verknüpft. Für die Gewaltwelle an amerikanischen Schulen zwischen 1985 und 1993 lässt sich ein solcher Zusammenhang auch nicht leugnen – diese »inner-city form of violence«[9] betraf vorwiegend die schwarzen Ghettos der Großstädte.[10] Die neue Gewaltwelle hingegen folgte einem »suburban-rural pattern«[11] und »erfasste [...] die Klein- und Vorstädte der amerikanischen Mittelschicht.«[12] Die Erklärungsversuche reichen in beiden Fällen von einem allgemeinen Werteverfall, über die Verherrlichung von Geld und Macht, die wachsende Kluft zwischen Reichen und der Mittelschicht, die Pop- und Videokultur bis hin zur Tendenz zur sofortigen Bedürfnisbefriedigung[13] – also Phänomene, die in den meisten modernen Industriestaaten anzutreffen sind und keineswegs typisch für Amerika sind.[14]

Die beiden anderen Argumente sind allerdings eindeutig Amerika-typisch. Seit ihrem Bestehen gelingt es der amerikanischen Waffenlobby – und an ihrer Spitze der National Rifle Association – Einschränkungen des Waffenbesitzes durch Privatpersonen zu verhindern. Aus offensichtlich wirtschaftlichen Gründen wird der Waffenbesitz zu einem Grundrecht erklärt wie etwa die Pressefreiheit oder das Recht der freien Meinungsäußerung. Wie selbstverständlich privater Waffenbesitz in den Vereinigten Staaten ist, sollen nur drei Beispiele belegen.[15] So heißt etwa der Beifahrersitz im Auto umgangssprachlich auch »shotgun seat«, in North Carolina ist im Eingangsbereich von Banken der Hinweis zu

---

9 *Deadly Lessons*, 2002, S. 303. Zitiert wird nach dem Internet-Vorabdruck des Berichts.
10 Vgl. Klingenstein, 2002.
11 *Deadly Lessons*, 2002, S. 303.
12 Klingenstein, 2002.
13 Vgl. ebd.
14 Die größere Zahl an Vorfällen kann auch eine Folge der größeren Bevölkerungszahl sein.
15 Vgl. auch Dick Flanagans Äußerung über den zweiten Verfassungszusatz auf S. 99.

finden, dass nur das Betreten mit einer verborgenen Schusswaffe verboten sei und nicht etwa mit einer Waffe überhaupt. Auch die ernst gemeinte Ansicht, privater Waffenbesitz könne Gewaltverbrecher abschrecken, ist nicht selten zu hören.[16] Offiziell begründet die NRA ihr Eintreten für ungehinderten privaten Waffenbesitz allerdings mit dem zweiten Verfassungszusatz in der Bill of Rights aus dem Jahr 1791. Als Motto zitiert die NRA auf ihrer Homepage diesen Zusatz wie folgt: »The right of the people to keep and bear arms, shall not be infringed« und ist damit in der Öffentlichkeit so erfolgreich, dass zur Rücknahme dieses Verfassungszusatzes die erforderliche Zweidrittelmehrheit im Repräsentantenhaus und im Senat[17] gegenwärtig nicht aufzubringen und auch eine entsprechende Entscheidung des Supreme Court nicht absehbar ist. Allerdings gibt es aus jüngster Zeit – wohl auch als Folge der Ereignisse in Littleton – in einigen amerikanischen Bundesstaaten Gerichtsentscheidungen niedrigerer Instanzen, die zu einer Einschränkung des Waffenbesitzes führen könnten. Ohne sich auf die Verfassungsdebatte einzulassen, ließ ein Appellationsgericht in Illinois Anfang 2002 eine Klage gegen Waffenhersteller wegen »Erregung öffentlichen Ärgernisses« als Folge der Überflutung des Marktes mit Feuerwaffen zu.[18] Da unter diesen Umständen Schadensersatzklagen betroffener Bürger in erheblicher Höhe zu erwarten sind, kommt der Entscheidung, sofern sie auf andere Bundesstaaten ausgedehnt und nicht von höheren Instanzen revidiert wird, eine ganz erhebliche praktische Bedeutung zu. Sie würde, ohne an den zweiten Verfassungszusatz zu rühren, zu einer drastischen Einschränkung des Waffenbesitzes führen – und sei es nur aus Furcht vor Schadensersatzklagen.[19]

16 Hingegen ist wohl eher das Gegenteil richtig. Ein Verbrecher, der mit gewaltsamer Gegenwehr zu rechnen hat, ist sicher eher zum Schusswaffengebrauch bereit als ein gesetzestreuer Bürger.

17 Die genauen Modalitäten einer Verfassungsänderung regelt Artikel 5 der Verfassung der Vereinigten Staaten.

18 Vgl. Julian Borger, »Ruling Gives Anti-gun Forces a Whiff of Victory«, in: *The Guardian*, 4.1.2002.

19 Vgl. auch S. 163 f., wo von freiwilligen Selbstbeschränkungen des Waffen-

Schließlich gibt es in den Vereinigten Staaten bereits seit langem eine Debatte über den zweiten Verfassungszusatz, der vollständig wie folgt lautet: »A well regulated Militia, being necessary to the security of a free State, the right of the people to keep and bear Arms, shall not be infringed.« Von besonderer Bedeutung ist hier der einleitende Kausalsatz – signifikanterweise von der NRA unterschlagen –, da in ihm die Voraussetzung für das Individualrecht auf uneingeschränkten Waffenbesitz genannt wird. Als 1791 die noch jungen Vereinigten Staaten den Zusatz in ihre Bill of Rights aufnahmen, geschah dies vor dem Hintergrund der erst 1783 errungenen staatlichen Unabhängigkeit. Ohne stehendes Heer hatten die Kolonien ihren Krieg gegen Großbritannien mit Hilfe einer Miliz geführt und gewonnen, die ohne privaten Waffenbesitz nicht denkbar war. Da aber, argumentieren die Befürworter der Einschränkung des privaten Waffenbesitzes, diese Voraussetzung nicht mehr gegeben sei, entfalle auch die Schlussfolgerung. Die Gegner jeder Einschränkung argumentieren jedoch – wenig überzeugend – damit, dass ein Kausalzusammenhang zwischen dem Bestehen einer Miliz und dem privaten Waffenbesitz nicht existiere. Welche dieser Auffassungen sich in Zukunft durchsetzen wird, ist im Augenblick nicht abzusehen.

2

In die komplexe Debatte um die Gründe für die Welle von Gewaltakten an amerikanischen Schulen schaltet sich auch Morton Rhue (d. i. Todd Strasser), der Autor des Aufsehen erregenden Jugendromans *The Wave* aus dem Jahr 1981, mit seinem Jugendroman *Give a Boy a Gun* ein, der bereits ein Jahr nach dem Amoklauf in Littleton erschien und mit der unzweideutigen politischen Aussage in der Widmung be-

herstellers Colt und von der Einführung des Abzugsschlosses in einigen amerikanischen Bundesstaaten die Rede ist.

ginnt: »[...] we live in a country where gun use and gun availability are horribly, insanely out of control.« Mit Ausnahme der einleitenden und abschließenden Abschnitte, in denen Rhue seine Absicht sowie neuere politische Entwicklungen darlegt, lässt der Autor den Roman auf der Arbeit einer Erzählerin basieren. Nach dem Tod eines der Täter, des fünfzehnjährigen Gary Searle, macht sich seine Stiefschwester, die zwanzigjährige Journalistikstudentin Denise Shipley,[20] daran, eine Chronik der fiktiven Ereignisse zusammenzustellen. Hierbei stützt sie sich jedoch nicht auf offizielle Polizeiberichte und Zeugenaussagen, sondern auf ihre eigenen Interviews mit Freunden, Mitschülern, Nachbarn und Lehrern, auf einige E-Mails und Chat-Protokolle, die sie auf Garys Computer findet, und belegt die zitierten Aussagen mit Auszügen aus tatsächlichen Publikationen.

Auf diese Weise entsteht ein Panorama der Ereignisse, das aus den unterschiedlichsten Perspektiven dargestellt wird, aber keine Objektivität beansprucht. Schließlich kann die Erzählerin von den Vorgängen nicht unberührt bleiben, weil ihr eigener Stiefbruder einer der Amokläufer ist und ihre Auswahl der zitierten Aussagen davon sicher nicht unbeeinflusst ist: »[Gary] wasn't a monster, just a boy who thought he'd run out of options. He was part of my life. I loved him; I still do« (S. 162). Es ist daher nicht verwunderlich, dass Gary in mehreren Aussagen als eher »lost and sad than angry« (S. 71) bzw. »weak and defenceless« (S. 72) dargestellt wird, vor dem Amoklauf lediglich für den Bombenbau und den Bombentest verantwortlich ist und Brendan schließlich von der konsequenten Beendigung der gemeinsam geplanten Geiselnahme abzubringen versucht. Damit aber nicht der Eindruck entstehen kann, es komme der Erzählerin vornehmlich auf eine Milderung der Schuld ihres Stiefbruders an, der durch den aggressiven Brendan Lawlor zu der Tat getrieben worden sei, nimmt sie in den Bericht

---

20 Auf eine genaue Darstellung der Familienverhältnisse wird nicht näher eingegangen. Denise kann Cynthias Tochter aus einer früheren Ehe sein.

nur solche Aussagen auf, die von den zahlreichen Drangsalierungen Brendans durch Mitschüler und Lehrer berichten und folglich als mildernde Umstände für Brendan gelten können. Von Gary wird dagegen nichts dergleichen berichtet. Trotz dieses offenkundigen Bemühens um Objektivität kann Denise jedoch ebenso wenig als Sprachrohr des Autors gelten wie die vielen anderen Zeugen, die sie zu Wort kommen lässt. Zum einen benutzen sie alle die Interviews nicht zuletzt, um ihre eigene Rolle zu rechtfertigen oder die Vorgänge zu verarbeiten, zum anderen vertreten sie so unterschiedliche Positionen, dass man sie als Charaktere eigenen Rechts betrachten kann.[21] Dem Leser ist es weitgehend überlassen, sich sein eigenes Bild von dem Geschehen und den Zusammenhängen zu machen. Für ihn gilt während der Lektüre, was Denise Shipley über die Bewohner von Middletown[22] berichtet: »Returning to Middletown was like stepping into a thick fog of bewilderment, fury, agony, and despair. For weeks I staggered through it, searching out other lost, wandering souls« (S. 11).[23]

3

Relativ einfach ist es noch, das Mosaik der Handlung aus den verschiedenen Aussagen zusammenzusetzen. Der Roman beginnt mit kurzen Porträts Brendans und Garys aus der Zeit, bevor der zwölfjährige Brendan als Siebtklässler mit seinen Eltern nach Middletown zieht. Bereits vor dem Wechsel auf die High School gehören beide zusammen mit den »Zeugen« Ryan Clancy und Allison Findley zu den Un-

---

21 Neben der hochaktuellen Thematik macht gerade diese Vielfältigkeit den Roman hervorragend einsetzbar für den Schulunterricht. Vgl. Abschnitt 4 des Nachworts.

22 Offenkundig ein »telling name«, der die Stadt als Durchschnittsort charakterisiert.

23 Erst außerhalb des eigentlichen Romans, in den »Final Thoughts«, meldet sich Morton Rhue wieder mit einem Appell an die jugendlichen Leser zu Wort (S. 173).

terprivilegierten, die sich dem Spott und den Nachstellungen der Clique um die Football-Spieler ausgesetzt sehen. Die Kette der verbalen und physischen, von den Lehrern weitgehend ignorierten Misshandlungen nimmt mit dem Wechsel auf die High School dramatische Formen an und kulminiert schließlich darin, dass Brendan von dem Football-Spieler Sam Flach während einer Party nahezu grundlos und brutal zusammengeschlagen wird (S. 102f.). Dieser Vorfall löst dann aus, was sich in gemeinsamen Gesprächen und E-Mails zwischen Gary und Brendan bereits verbal und in einer Reihe von Aktionen zunehmend angekündigt hat: Gary und Brendan nutzen die Gelegenheit eines Tanzabends in der Turnhalle der Schule, um an den Ausgängen Sprengladungen anzubringen, alle Anwesenden als Geiseln zu nehmen und die Lehrer, Männer und älteren Schüler zu fesseln. Es kommt zwar im weiteren Verlauf nicht zu Morden, wohl aber wird Allen Curry, der Direktor der Schule, angeschossen, und Sam Flach wird durch Schüsse in die Knie zum Krüppel geschossen. Allison Findley, eine Freundin der Täter und überraschend zugegen, rettet Sam Flach das Leben, indem sie ihm aus Gürteln ihrer Mitschüler Verbände anlegt, die den Blutverlust stoppen. Der Polizei gelingt es nicht, die Geiselnahme zu beenden. Erst als Paul Burns und Dustin Williams ihre Fesseln lösen können und Gary Selbstmord begeht, überwältigt Dustin Williams Brendan und die Geiseln können befreit werden. In der Folge nehmen einige Geiseln brutale Rache an Brendan. Obwohl Dustin Williams, Allison Findley sowie die Beratungslehrerin Beth Bender sich ihnen entgegenstellen, verletzen sie ihn so schwer, dass er irreparable Gehirnschäden davonträgt und im Koma liegt.

Lässt sich also die Handlung relativ leicht rekonstruieren, wirft die Frage nach der Allgemeingültigkeit der Ereignisse größere Probleme auf. Zwar ist Middletown offenbar eine typische amerikanische Kleinstadt, doch sind die Verhältnisse an der Middletown High School durchaus nicht charakteristisch für alle amerikanischen Schulen. Hier scheint die Rolle der sportlich aktiven und erfolgreichen Schüler – vornehmlich der Football-Spieler – ungleich stärker ausgeprägt zu sein als an anderen Schulen. Zumindest lassen die Aussagen Chelsea Bakers, die erst zu Beginn der zehnten Klasse auf die Middletown High School wechselt, darauf schließen:

>It's so different from my old school. You expect it to be different, but what surprised me was the *way* it was different. It's just a lot more rigid here. It's like, are you in the popular crowd or not? There was a popular crowd at my old school, too, but they were still nice to most people. They didn't act like if you weren't one of them you didn't deserve to exist< (S. 79).

und: >But here, it's like the only thing that matters is sports. You get straight A's and people dump on you. It doesn't make sense< (S. 89).

Die Football-Spieler – allen voran Sam Flach – rechtfertigen ihre privilegierte Rolle an der Schule damit, dass sie mit ihren Erfolgen zum >school spirit< beitrügen, womit offenbar der auf sportlichen Erfolgen basierende Ruf der Schule in der Öffentlichkeit gemeint ist. Für einige der Sportler, so der Englischlehrer Dick Flanagan, seien akademische Erfolge in der Tat weniger wichtig: >A great season here may be the highlight of their life. But even if it isn't, the lessons they learn about work and discipline will serve them well in whatever they do< (S. 89).[24] Mit dieser Aussage rechtfertigt er implizit die Sonderrolle der Football-Spieler, aber natürlich nicht deren Übergriffe und Disziplinlosigkeiten. Für akademische Erfolge der Schüler verwendet er dagegen eher den Begriff >school pride< (S. 82). Beide Begriffe hätten an einer Schule ihren Platz, und die Schule, so Flanagans Argumentation, könne für die Ereignisse nicht verantwortlich gemacht werden (S. 153). Die nicht privilegierten Schüler hingegen sehen weniger den Beitrag der Football-Spieler und ihrer Anhänger zum Ruf der Schule als vielmehr die Ungerechtig-

24 Auch Beth Bender vertritt die These von der wichtigen Rolle des Sports bei der Persönlichkeitsentwicklung von Jugendlichen (S. 44).

keit einer ungleichen Behandlung. Sportler an der Middletown High School scheinen sich so gut wie alles erlauben zu dürfen. Sowohl Disziplinlosigkeit im Schulalltag als auch ihre verbalen und physischen Angriffe auf Mitschüler bleiben ungeahndet.

Zwar ist also einer der Gründe für die dramatische Zuspitzung der Ereignisse in der spezifischen Situation an der Middletown High School und weniger in der amerikanischen Schulsituation im Allgemeinen zu suchen, doch reicht dieses Erklärungsmuster allein nicht aus. Selbst an dieser so durch den Sport geprägten Schule sind Grenzüberschreitungen gelegentlich möglich. Der Afro-Amerikaner Dustin Williams wird seinerseits wegen seiner guten sportlichen und akademischen Erfolge allgemein anerkannt, ist aber auch einer der wenigen Vertrauten von Brendan; und Emily Kirsch, einer Freundin von Brendan, gelingt es, von der Gruppe der populären Schüler akzeptiert zu werden. Da Dustin und Emily auch eingestehen, dass Gary und Brendan durch ihr eigenes Verhalten gegenüber der Sportlerfraktion zum Widerspruch reizen (S. 81, 87 f.), liegt es nahe, Gründe für Garys und Brendans Tat auch in ihren Charakteranlagen zu suchen.

4

Zur Beurteilung der Protagonisten können vornehmlich die beiden Abschiedsbriefe, die im Verlauf des Romans abschnittsweise vorgestellt und erst vor den letzten beiden Kapiteln vollständig abgedruckt werden, sowie die Auszüge aus ihren E-Mails und Chats und schließlich die Aussagen ihrer Freunde, Feinde und Lehrer herangezogen werden. Aus den Abschiedsbriefen spricht die tiefe Verzweiflung zweier Jugendlicher, die sich durch die Gefühllosigkeit und Intoleranz ihrer Umwelt zu ihrer Tat gezwungen sehen. Die – letztlich nicht begangenen – Morde will Gary als Fanal verstanden wissen, das die Bevölkerung zu mehr Toleranz veranlassen soll.[25] »Maybe something will change, and some other miserable kid like me will get treated better and maybe find a reason to live« (S. 117f.), heißt es in Garys Abschiedsbrief an seine Mutter. Brendans Brief dagegen ist Ausdruck seines Hasses auf die Gesellschaft, die Außenseiter nicht akzeptiert, und spricht nur von Vergeltung für erlittenes Unrecht: »Well, screw you. Screw all of you. I hope this letter is a knife in your hearts. You ruined my life. All I've done is pay you back in kind« (S. 134).[26] Dieser Eindruck wird auch durch die E-Mail- und Chat-Protokolle bestätigt. Brendans Sprache ist ebenso vulgär, wie sein Rachedurst zügellos ist. Bereits ein Jahr vor der Tat offenbart er in seinen E-Mails Mordgedanken an Sam Flach und dem Biologielehrer F. Douglas Ellin. Sam Flach verspricht er einen langsamen, qualvollen Tod (S. 40), seinem Lehrer droht er an »[to pop] a cap in his ass with a friggin' TEC-9« (S. 46), und wenig später sieht er sich als Rächer aller Unterprivilegierten (S. 66). Gary hingegen zeigt sich in den Chat-Protokollen, in denen er den Namen Dayzd trägt, als im höchsten Maß orientierungslos, als *dazed*, also »verwirrt«. Das Attentat in Littleton führt er zunächst auf bloße Orientierungslosigkeit und Langeweile der Täter zurück: »Nothing better 2 do« (S. 74) und glaubt noch an die Möglichkeit einer engen zwischenmenschlichen Bindung, bevor er gegen Ende des Gesprächs Brendans Auffassung teilt, die Mörder von Littleton hätten mit ihrer Tat ein Zeichen setzen wollen und man solle es ihnen deshalb gleichtun. Die Äußerungen lassen sich auch nicht als das pubertäre Gerede Vierzehn- bzw. Fünfzehnjähriger abtun, weil diesen Worten auch rasch Taten folgen. Zunächst erschreckt Brendan Autofahrer damit, dass er vorgibt, von einer Straßenbrücke Gegenstände auf die Fahrbahn zu werfen, dann schießt er bei einer Autofahrt auf Gegenstände, und schließlich baut Gary

25 Von Selbstmord spricht Gary offenbar schon ein Jahr vor der Tat (S. 50).
26 An dem grundsätzlichen Misstrauen gegenüber Außenseitern ändert sich auch nach den Ereignissen nichts. Ryan Clancys und Allison Findleys Spinde werden insgeheim regelmäßig auf Verdächtiges hin untersucht (S. 157).

eine Bombe, die er und seine Freunde in einem einsamen Waldgelände testen. Das Attentat auf die Schule ist danach nur noch eine unvermeidliche Konsequenz aus der allmählichen Überwindung des Gewalttabus.

Obwohl Garys und Brendans sadistisches und brutales Verhalten während der Geiselnahme jede Form von Sympathie des Lesers mit ihnen unmöglich macht, gibt es doch bei beiden Tätern Indizien dafür, dass sie nicht von Natur aus gefühllos sind. Besonders deutlich sind die Indizien hierfür im Fall des nach außen hin so kalten und brutalen Brendan. Nach dem Umzug nach Middletown offenbart seine Reaktion auf das Hilfsangebot seiner Lehrerin Brendans tiefes Bedürfnis nach Zuwendung und Verständnis, und auch in seinem langen Gespräch mit Dustin Williams kann er kaum seine Tränen zurückhalten: »Maybe it was my imagination, but I thought his eyes were glistening, like with tears« (S. 153).[27] Offenbar haben seine Eltern, die als nett, sympathisch, aber auch überfordert dargestellt werden, keinen Zugang zu ihrem Sohn. Brendan versteckt seine emotionalen Bedürfnisse hinter einer rauen Schale – und dies auf die Dauer so vollständig, dass sich aus seiner inneren Zerrissenheit letztlich ein abgrundtiefer Hass auf die Gesellschaft und der Wunsch nach Rache entwickeln. Dick Flanagan erkennt die Zerrissenheit Brendans bereits im neunten Schuljahr, wenn er von ihm berichtet: »You see kids like him every year. You get the feeling they're at war in their mind, fighting some constant battle within themselves as well as with everyone around them« (S. 53).

Auch ihre besten Freunde Ryan Clancy und Allison Findley, die ebenfalls zu den Außenseitern gehören und einen großen Teil der Freizeit mit ihnen verbringen, können Brendan und Gary nicht positiv beeinflussen. Sie stellen zum einen die wichtigste Informationsquelle für die Erzählerin dar,

---

27 Für Gary wäre in diesem Zusammenhang an die Szene mit Allison im Auto seiner Eltern zu erinnern, bei der es zu einem von Sam Flach und Deirdre Bunson beobachteten ersten vorsichtigen Austausch von Zärtlichkeiten kommt (S. 33).

zum andern besteht ihre weitere Hauptfunktion darin, den nahe liegenden Schluss zu widerlegen, der häufige Alkohol- und Drogengenuss sowie die Computer- und Videokultur trügen die Hauptschuld an der Entwicklung. Schließlich finden sich Gary und Allison mit ihrer Rolle ab, ohne zu Gewalttaten zu neigen, obwohl sie im Wesentlichen den gleichen Freizeitaktivitäten nachgehen wie Brendan und Gary. Im Gegenteil – Allison spielt bei der Befreiung der Geiseln und der Rettung Sam Flachs vor dem Verbluten eine entscheidende Rolle: »I'm not sure I believe in miracles, but ever since that night, I definitely believe in angels. Only you never know who they might be or what form they might take. If Allison Findley could be an angel, anyone could« (S. 142).[28]

Auch die Lehrer können keinen positiven Einfluss auf die beiden Täter nehmen – am wenigsten natürlich der Sportlehrer Bosco, der mit seinen Football-Spielern gemeinsame Sache macht. Der Direktor der Schule, Allen Curry, wird seiner Rolle nicht gerecht, weil er in erster Linie seine Aufgabe darin sieht, der Öffentlichkeit ein »Produkt« zu liefern, das sie wünscht. Die Schule könne nicht die Rolle des Elternhauses übernehmen, den Jugendlichen Wertvorstellungen und Orientierungen zu vermitteln:

> »Running a school is like running a business. I know this may sound crass, but you're producing a product. In our case, that product is a high school senior who is prepared to go on in the world and be successful in the community. So, in a way, you can say that we have to produce a product that the community approves of, that they will buy into« (S. 89 f.).

Bei einer solchen konformistischen Grundeinstellung bleiben natürlich Außenseiter und Individualisten wie Brendan, Gary, Ryan und Allison auf der Strecke. Erziehung zu sozia-

---

28 Ryan ist bei der Geiselnahme aus nicht genannten Gründen abwesend.

ler Anpassung statt zu Individualität und Toleranz ist Currys Motto.[29]

Die einzigen Lehrer, in denen die Ereignisse zumindest nachträglich eine Erkenntnis wecken, die Erfolg bei dem Kampf gegen die Gewaltbereitschaft an Schulen verspricht, sind Beth Bender und F. Douglas Ellin. Zwar gelingt es auch Beth Bender nicht, Zugang zu Brendan zu gewinnen (S. 37f.), und wird Ellin zu Brendans bevorzugtem Hassobjekt, weil er ihn nicht vor einem relativ harmlosen Übergriff Sam Flachs schützt (S. 45f.), aber zumindest könnte die Umsetzung ihrer Einsichten für die Zukunft eine Verbesserung der Situation herbeiführen.

5

Hierzu ist zunächst eine genaue Diagnose der Gründe für die Gewalt an Schulen erforderlich. Die von der Erzählerin gesammelten Aussagen zu diesem Aspekt werden – abgesetzt vom eigentlichen Romantext und in einem anderen Schrifttyp gedruckt – wirkungsvoll unterstützt durch die Zitate aus den verschiedensten, meist journalistischen oder offiziellen Quellen. Allein 54 dieser Auszüge beschäftigen sich mit dem Problem der leichten Verfügbarkeit und der zunehmenden Bereitschaft zum Einsatz von Feuerwaffen und treten eindeutig für eine Erschwerung des individuellen Zugangs zu Waffen ein. Das allein kann jedoch das Problem nicht beseitigen. So hat etwa das Verbot des Besitzes von Handfeuerwaffen in Großbritannien keineswegs zu einem Rückgang der Gewaltverbrechen geführt,[30] weil sich tendenziell zur Gewaltanwendung neigende Straftäter kaum von

29 In dieses Bild passt auch sein unreflektiertes populistisches Eintreten für die Beibehaltung des ungehinderten individuellen Zugangs zu Schusswaffen (S. 127f.), das er im Übrigen mit Dick Flanagan teilt, der jeden Eingriff in die Verfassung strikt ablehnt (S. 99f.).
30 Im Januar 2000 berichtete BBC-Online, dass die Zahl der bewaffneten Raubüberfälle innerhalb eines Jahres um 19% gestiegen sei.

gesetzlichen Vorschriften abhalten lassen. Weitere 23 Auszüge behandeln andere Gründe wie den Einfluss der Medienkultur, den allgemeinen Werteverlust Jugendlicher als Folge des Fehlens von Rollenvorbildern, die zunehmende Abkehr von traditionellen religiösen Werten, das Cliquenwesen an Schulen, aber auch individual-psychologische Probleme der Täter.[31]

Unbestreitbar ist zunächst einmal die wachsende gesellschaftliche Isolierung Jugendlicher durch die neuen Medien, die den realen kommunikativen Kontakt mit Mitmenschen durch virtuellen Kontakt ersetzen – etwa durch Videospiele, E-Mails, SMS-Nachrichten und Chatrooms. Weniger offensichtlich ist jedoch der Zusammenhang zwischen der Nutzung dieser Medien und der Gewaltanwendung. Offizielle Untersuchungen in den Vereinigten Staaten deuten immerhin an, dass in der Tat ein solcher ursächlicher Zusammenhang besteht.[32]

Weitere fünf Auszüge bestätigen den zunehmenden Werteverlust Jugendlicher, entweder weil die Erwachsenen wie etwa Cynthia Searle oder Samantha Lawlor trotz großer Anstrengungen keinen Zugang zu ihren Kindern finden oder ihn gar nicht erst suchen und stattdessen die Heranwachsenden mit ihren Problemen allein lassen, wie Professor William Damon von der Stanford University schreibt:

»There has never […] been a cohort of kids that is so little affected by adult guidance and so attuned to a peer world. […] We have removed grown-up wisdom and allowed [children] to drift into a self-constructed, highly relativistic world of friendship and peers« (S. 79).

In diesem Zusammenhang wird auch zweimal die Abkehr der Jugendlichen von religiösen Werten genannt. In dem Ro-

---

31 Diese Gründe nennt auch die Studie *Deadly Lessons*, 2002, S. 301 ff.
32 Vgl. Klingenstein, 2002. Über die praktischen Folgen des Mediengebrauchs jeglicher Art wird seit langem erbittert gestritten. Erinnert sei nur an die zahlreichen Zensurgesetze, die unliebsame Kunstwerke verbieten sollen, weil man deren schädliche Folgen fürchtet.

mantext selbst bekennen sich Gary und Brendan zum Atheismus, andererseits vertritt Chelsea Baker mit großer Selbstverständlichkeit die christliche Position der Nächstenliebe: »The Lord says we should do unto others as we would have them do unto us. It's not very complicated« (S. 145), und sie bewertet Dustins mutiges Eingreifen nicht als Heldentum, sondern schlicht als moralische Pflicht: »It's what a moral human being is supposed to do« (S. 147).[33]

Weitere acht Auszüge aus Quellen schließlich befassen sich mit dem Problem der Cliquenbildung an Schulen. An der Columbine High School in Littleton schienen 1999 ähnliche Zustände zu herrschen wie im fiktionalen Middletown: »Like most students, I lived in fear of the small slights and public humiliations used to reinforce the rigid high school caste system: Poor girls were sluts, soft boys were fags« (S. 39).

Aus diesem Bündel von Gründen für den Gewaltausbruch in Middletown ziehen in dem Roman einzig Beth Bender, F. Douglas Ellin und Denise Shipley wichtige therapeutische Konsequenzen. Beth Bender erkennt, dass der fehlende Minderheitenschutz Gary und Brendan zu ihrer Tat getrieben hat. Ohne das Verbrechen zu entschuldigen, kann sie doch ein gewisses Verständnis für die Motive der beiden nicht verhehlen, und sie ist davon überzeugt, dass es Aufgabe der Schulen ist, sich der Tendenz zur Gewaltanwendung entgegenzustellen. Dazu gehört ihrer Ansicht nach auch die Einschränkung des individuellen Waffenbesitzes, weil emotional und psychisch gefährdete Jugendliche in Extremsituationen zur Waffe greifen könnten. Auch Douglas Ellin besteht darauf, dass Schulen ein Hort der Sicherheit für alle Schüler sein müssen. Er akzeptiert zwar aus biologischen Gründen die Existenz einer hierarchischen Hackordnung, besteht aber aus sozialen Gründen darauf, dass die Erwachsenen zum Schutz der Minderheiten verpflichtet seien:

33 Dieser Appell zur Rückkehr zu traditionell christlichen Werten darf zwar nicht übersehen werden, nimmt jedoch in dem Roman keineswegs eine zentrale Position ein.

»Teasing, bullying, fighting – these are how children establish their pecking order. It is, unfortunately, natural for children to do this. And it is the responsibility of adults to supervise and stop this behavior. One thing that is wrong with our schools is that we are permitting too much of the former and not enough of the latter« (S. 157).

Denise Shipley schließlich fordert eine Einschränkung des individuellen Zugangs zu Handfeuerwaffen sowie größere Toleranz gegenüber Andersdenkenden – eine Auffassung, die auch Morton Rhue selbst in seinen »Final Thoughts« teilt. Eine ähnliche Ansicht vertritt auch die bereits öfter zitierte Studie der amerikanischen National Academy of Science. Aus den beiden Gewaltwellen an amerikanischen Schulen – zuerst in den verwahrlosten *inner cities* der Großstädte und später in den amerikanischen Kleinstädten der Mittelschicht – könne man lernen, dass der Zugang Jugendlicher zu Waffen erschwert werden müsse, aber auch, dass es Aufgabe der Gesellschaft sei, Hilfsbedürftigen beizustehen, die ihre Stellung in der Gesellschaft bedroht sehen:

»To become and remain a nation that creates equal opportunity for all, that creates the conditions under which individuals can make the most of their talents in whatever pursuit interests them, communities must help young people get to the starting line of adult life with health, vitality, and confidence. Communities that cannot keep their children safe from lethal violence, that endure conditions in which those reaching for adult status and competence in schools cannot be safe, are failing to protect the American dream.«[34]

Für die Mithilfe bei der Erstellung des Glossars, die gründliche Durchsicht des Manuskripts sowie das Korrekturlesen bedanke ich mich bei Bettina Drawe aus Essen.

Herbert Geisen

34 *Deadly Lessons*, 2002, S. 302.

Inhalt

Give a Boy a Gun   3

Editorische Notiz 176
Literaturhinweise 177
Nachwort 178

Fremdsprachentexte

IN RECLAMS UNIVERSAL-BIBLIOTHEK

Amerikanische Literatur (Auswahl)

Edward Albee: Who's Afraid of Virginia Woolf? 206 S. UB 9073

America. A Reader. 352 S. UB 19719

American Love Stories. 208 S. UB 9097

American Crime Stories. 167 S. UB 9268

American Political Speeches. 175 S. UB 9137

Paul Auster: City of Glass. 248 S. UB 9078 – Moon Palace. 456 S. UB 9083

L. Frank Baum: The Wonderful Wizard of Oz. 211 S. UB 9001

Ambrose Bierce: The Devil's Dictionary. 157 S. UB 9057

Robert Bloch: Psycho. 239 S. UB 9066

T. C. Boyle: After the Plague and Other Stories. 239 S. UB 9149

Ray Bradbury: Fahrenheit 451. 247 S. UB 9270 – The Martian Chronicles. 338 S. UB 9058

Bill Bryson: Notes from a Big Country. 172 S. UB 9134

Howard Buten: When I Was Five I Killed Myself. 214 S. UB 9100

Ernest Callenbach: Ecotopia. 367 S. UB 9030

Raymond Carver: Short Cuts. 237 S. UB 9079

Truman Capote: Breakfast at Tiffany's. 157 S. UB 9241 – Hand-carved Coffins. 144 S. UB 9110

Raymond Chandler: The Big Sleep. 379 S. UB 9009 – Killer in the Rain. 128 S. UB 9198

Contemporary American Short Stories. 155 S. UB 9206

Stephen Crane: Maggie: A Girl of the Streets. 135 S. UB 9289

Bob Dylan: Lyrics. 155 S. UB 19741

F. Scott Fitzgerald: The Great Gatsby. 255 S. UB 9242

Winston Groom: Forrest Gump. 301 S. UB 9033

Ernest Hemingway: The Old Man and the Sea. 140 S. UB 9075 – The Snows of Kilimanjaro. Six Stories. 176 S. UB 9120

Patricia Highsmith: A Shot from Nowhere. Six Stories. 160 S. UB 9262 – The Talented Mr. Ripley. 437 S. UB 9145

Denis Johnson: Jesus' Son. 157 S. UB 9092

Kressmann Taylor: Address Unknown. 63 S. UB 9107

Cormac McCarthy: The Road. 296 S. UB 19757

Nick McDonell: Twelve. 237 S. UB 9127

Herman Melville: Bartleby. 88 S. UB 9190

Arthur Miller: Death of a Salesman. 171 S. UB 9172 – The Crucible. 224 S. UB 9257

Mexican-American Short Stories. 179 S. UB 9124

Modern American Short Stories. 160 S. UB 9216

New York Fiction. 154 S. UB 9070

Eugene O'Neill: Long Day's Journey into Night. 216 S. UB 9252

Edgar Allan Poe: The Gold-Bug and Other Tales. 192 S. UB 9173 – The Murders in the Rue Morgue. 80 S. UB 9088

Morton Rhue: Give a Boy a Gun. 195 S. UB 9111

Philip Roth: Everyman. 207 S. UB 19751

John Steinbeck: Of Mice and Men. 173 S. UB 9253 – Tortilla Flat. 280 S. UB 9027

James Thurber: Stories and Fables of Our Time. Ill. 88 S. UB 9232

West Side Story. A Musical. (Jerome Robbins / Arthur Laurents / Leonard Bernstein / Stephen Sondheim.) 136 S. UB 9212

Thornton Wilder: The Bridge of San Luis Rey. 152 S. UB 9195 – Our Town. 127 S. UB 9168

Tennessee Williams: Cat on a Hot Tin Roof. 223 S. UB 9039 – The Glass Menagerie. 149 S. UB 9178 – A Streetcar Named Desire. 199 S. UB 9240

Philipp Reclam jun. Stuttgart

Fremdsprachentexte

IN RECLAMS UNIVERSAL-BIBLIOTHEK

Englische Prosa

Douglas Adams: *The Hitchhiker's Guide to the Galaxy*. 320 S. UB 19744

British Political Speeches. From Churchill to Blair. 190 S. UB 9084

Anthony Burgess: *A Clockwork Orange*. 261 S. UB 9281

Lewis Carroll: *Alice's Adventures in Wonderland*. Ill. 165 S. UB 9160

Bruce Chatwin: *In Patagonia*. 379 S. UB 9099

Joseph Conrad: *Heart of Darkness*. 189 S. UB 9161

Roald Dahl: *Three Tales of the Unexpected*. 96 S. UB 9215 – *The Witches*. 192 S. UB 9080

Charles Dickens: *A Christmas Carol*. 155 S. UB 9150

Garry Disher: *The Apostle Bird*. 152 S. UB 9101

Arthur Conan Doyle: *The Speckled Band*. Four Sherlock Holmes Stories. 184 S. UB 9003

Daphne Du Maurier: *The Birds*. 76 S. UB 9287 – *Don't Look Now*. 109 S. UB 9054

English Literature. From Chaucer to McEwan. 311 S. UB 9123

English Proverbs. 152 S. UB 9235

Graham Gardner: *Inventing Elliot*. 267 S. UB 19720

Nadine Gordimer: *Town and Country Lovers. Three Stories*. 96 S. UB 9237

Graffiti. 88 S. UB 9112

Graham Greene: *The Third Man*. 173 S. UB 9180

Aldous Huxley: *Brave New World*. 323 S. UB 9284

Kazuo Ishiguro: *The Remains of the Day*. 373 S. UB 9138

James Joyce: *Dubliners*. A Selection. 104 S. UB 9181

Judith Kerr: *When Hitler Stole Pink Rabbit*. 268 S. UB 9076

Doris Lessing: *To Room Nineteen*. 72 S. UB 9151

London Stories. 228 S. UB 9106

London Underground. Poems and Prose About the Tube. 199 S. UB 9104

Katherine Mansfield: *The Garden-Party*. Five Short Stories. 85 S. UB 9152

W. Somerset Maugham: *The Letter*. 75 S. UB 9183

Ian McEwan: *The Cement Garden*. 182 S. UB 9069 – *The Daydreamer*. 160 S. UB 9119 – *On Chesil Beach*. 199 S. UB 19754

A. A. Milne: *Winnie-the-Pooh*. Ill. 180 S. UB 9231

Mini-Sagas. *An Anthology of Fifty-Word Short Stories*. 183 S. UB 9146

Salman Rushdie: *East, West*. 275 S. UB 9094

Alan Sillitoe: *The Loneliness of the Long-distance Runner*. 88 S. UB 9192 – *Saturday Night and Sunday Morning*. 360 S. UB 9038

Muriel Spark: *The Prime of Miss Jean Brodie*. 189 S. UB 9193

Robert Louis Stevenson: *The Bottle Imp*. 59 S. UB 9157 – *The Strange Case of Dr. Jekyll and Mr. Hyde*. 119 S. UB 9167

Think more, act less. English aphorisms. 148 S. UB 9296

Urban Legends. 104 S. UB 9065

Evelyn Waugh: *The Loved One*. 192 S. UB 9233

H. G. Wells: *The Time Machine*. 160 S. UB 9176

Oscar Wilde: *The Canterville Ghost*. 64 S. UB 9177 – *The Happy Prince and Other Tales*. 91 S. UB 9293 – *The Picture of Dorian Gray*. 344 S. UB 9019

Virginia Woolf: *Mrs Dalloway's Party*. A Short Story Sequence. 96 S. UB 9196

Philipp Reclam jun. Stuttgart